The Conscience

of the

Community

by

Rev. George Walker Smith

with

Francine Phillips

Copyright, 2002

Write Now!
write.now@cox.net

Author: Rev. George Walker Smith
Co-author: Francine Phillips
Cover Design: Deneen Powell Atelier Inc.
Foreword: Herb Klein

ISBN: 9637698-2-0

Table of Contents

Acknowledgements

I am honored and grateful to my book collaborator, Francine Phillips, who spent an enormous amount of time articulating each aspect of my biography, and to Dr. Stephen Weber, president of San Diego State University, who enabled me to publish this book. In addition, I appreciate the many expressions of appreciation by folks of all races and cultures who were good to me throughout my life's journey and who deserve to share part of the book's credit.

Special thanks to my beloved wife, Irene, and my children, Carolyn, Joyce and Anthony. My family patiently shared my life experiences as a husband and father. They supported my passion as a Presbyterian minister as well as my lifelong commitment to my community.

I must acknowledge my wonderful mother, Amanda, for providing me the special love, guidance and wisdom that contributed to my personal growth and development for many years to come.

My life experiences have taught me many things, but one thing I have seen confirmed over and over is the need for all youth to obtain an education. I believe that education is absolutely vital to one's personal freedom. I also believe that people have a responsibility to treat each other with respect and compassion without racial prejudice. The source of prejudice is ignorance and ignorance, again, obstructs freedom.

In appreciation for the help I received along the way from so many people in this world and the next, I dedicate the essence of this book to our community's youth, who will be the primary architects at the dawn of a new society.

I continue to believe that in America, you can achieve your life's goals by believing in yourself and who you are. A healthy and sustained faith in God will also guide you through many of life's challenges and experiences in ways that you could never imagine.

"Go forth, and make your mark in life!"

Reverend George Walker Smith, 2002

5

Forword

Most would say, "He is his own man."

Others observe, "You never know exactly where he is coming from."

Whatever the comment, the San Diego leader known as "the Reverend," has never been one to withhold his opinions.

Many know him as an African-American who has been a Republican leader in San Diego for over forty years. His activities are multifold: the organizer and chairman of The Catfish Club, a group feared by many politicians (but a group they cannot ignore); a wise religious leader; a member of the San Diego Board of Education for sixteen years; a board member of more than twenty San Diego organizations. These and many other phrases describe George Walker Smith.

As the title of this book illustrates, he is a man dedicated to being a "conscience of the community."

My friendship with George covers about fifty years, almost from the time he arrived in San Diego with a new Ford, a wonderful bride, a new church, and a mission to build a better life for his parishioners. A few years later, I still can remember the then-young educator coming by my office to share the excitement he enjoyed as the first African-American to be elected to the school board. Over the years, I never have found him lacking in constructive ideas.

In this autobiography, Smith quotes from Exodus 4:12 where the Lord says to Moses, "Now, therefore, go and I will be with your mouth and teach you what you will speak." Moses resisted at first, but not Smith, who describes himself as the "Little Black Moses" from highly segregated Lowdes County, Alabama. George speaks out. And no one in years has tried to teach him how to express himself. Not even Moses would have dared.

When he speaks, people don't always agree, but they do listen.

The surprise of *Conscience of the Community* comes not in Smith's views or his many accomplishments. The book is particularly revealing as Smith discusses his childhood, an interesting

7

and important part of his life unknown to most of his friends.

Smith makes it clear he believes God's direction changed his life from that of a sharecropper to a religious and community leader. I believe we are fortunate that God brought him to San Diego. It is my opinion that the clarity and strength of his views have been a key factor in dispelling racial uprisings in our city.

It becomes even clearer in this autobiography that Smith will continue to be a "conscience of the community." He will be the quiet mentor for many and the outspoken leader of his beloved Catfish Club. He would humbly admit that he may not always be right in his views, but he will always be a passionate advocate for his beliefs. He is persuasive, and his batting average is high.

He can be rough. He can be stubborn. He can be humorous. He is not afraid to swim upstream. Because he is fair-minded and has earned deep respect from both blacks and whites, he has been a leader in building understanding between races in San Diego.

That is George Walker Smith, a man who has brought to his community a lifelong legacy of achievement eloquently described in the pages of this autobiography.

Herbert G. Klein, Vice President and Editor-in-Chief
Copley Newspapers

John E. Farrior, Haynesville, Alabama, 1942

Section One

Little Black Moses

Chapter One

In Pharoah's Palace

In dark and hidden rooms, hot with humidity and seeping with the clean sweat of hard-working Negroes, mixed with the unclean nervous sweat of fear, a small group of men met secretly to discuss the struggle for human rights in Alabama. It was the late 1950s and the complex fits and starts of the fledgling civil rights revolution had reached the point where solidarity was absolutely necessary. Rosa Parks had just been arrested in Montgomery, Alabama, for not sitting at the back of the bus after a long day of work. A champion was needed.

The first choice, and my number one hero of modern history, was Edward Nixon, a Pullman porter from Montgomery County, Alabama. His profession had long been involved in equal rights, since the organization of the Brotherhood of Sleeping Car Porters in 1925. I had first heard of him in 1942, at the age of 13, when I began to notice the whispers of Negroes who were willing to stand up against oppression and injustice, just as I heard whispers of lynching and murder, rapes and raids, by hooded Klansmen throughout my childhood.

For years Ed Nixon had been the leader of black causes. Long before Rosa Parks refused to move to the back of the bus, Ed Nixon had been tackling unjust power structures. When a Negro was unjustly treated, there would be a visit from Ed Nixon to the local authorities. He would not stand by, but would speak out. How did he get away with it? Ed Nixon was not afraid of the devil. By the late '50s he was an unofficial spokesman for what was then called "Negro America." And Negro America was saying, "Enough is enough."

When Rosa Parks was arrested, people naturally turned to Ed Nixon to lead a boycott of the buses in Alabama and to be the spokesman for the cause.

"I don't have the education," he countered. It was a convincing argument. Education has always been of great value to the black community because it was forbidden. "Go after that new young pastor of the Dexter Avenue Baptist Church," said Nixon. "Young Martin. He has the education to lead."

So the delegation parted and crept back into the Alabama night. Later they met with Martin Luther King and his son, young Martin Jr., and it was decided that the new pastor would become the spokesman for civil rights in the South. Rosa Parks, who had participated in several civil rights actions prior to her famous bus ride, Edward Nixon, Rev. Vernon Johns, and Rev. Martin Luther King, Jr. were all part of a movement of unity among Negroes in Alabama that had been growing since the first Freedom Riders bought their bus tickets in 1947, the same year Jackie Robinson broke the color barrier as a member of the Brooklyn Dodgers.

I was the same age as Martin Luther King Jr. By the time the municipal bus laws in Montgomery were overturned in 1955, I was preaching the gospel of equality in Pittsburgh. God would soon direct my civil rights struggle down a different road, which led 3,000 miles away. It was a road I had been walking on for as far back as I could remember.

* * *

The day was hot, dusty and humid when I set out with my brother Henry to the General Store. The gravel road wound past the fields alive with prickly cotton, taller than we were. Although I was only eight years old, and younger than Henry, I had list of provisions and was in charge of the shopping. I walked with a sense of purpose as Henry loped alongside. I could read. I could read my list.

Ever since I was a small boy I had picked up pieces of paper discarded along that road – letters, pamphlets – particularly the Watchtower pamphlets from the Jehovah's Witnesses. Anything written down on paper drew me to pick it up, dust it off and read the words. Information still enthralls me; today I read seven newspapers every morning. Back then, in the town where I grew up, it was not only unusual for a black child to love reading, but for any child to crave the written word. I was different.

Hayneville, Alabama, was like most Southern towns during the Depression. It was the county seat of Lowndes County, which had the richest black soil and the poorest black people in the United States of America. Negroes outnumbered white people seven to one, and if we had been the least bit visible, it might have posed a threat to the established power structure. But for the most part, Negroes were invisible, part of the land we sweated over, part of the floors we cleaned – no more significant than a kitchen appliance or a farming tool.

In Hayneville, and throughout most of the South, Negroes had no economic rights to open bank accounts or carry on commerce. Our money, if we had any, was kept in cloth pouches, hidden. We had no voting rights – the rules were determined not by ballots, but by a history of oppression and a tradition of illiteracy and ignorance. We had no money, no police protection, no social standing, no political power, no education and no hope. As a Negro, you were never allowed to have a gun and you couldn't kill a deer even if you were starving.

Injustice was our meat; fear was our milk.

We were sharecroppers at a plantation on the outskirts of Hayneville owned by the Farrior family. Sharecropping was a la-

14

bor system that grew out of the reparations after the Civil War and the Emancipation Proclamation. It was hated by both whites and blacks.

Many young slaves who were smuggled out of the South during the Civil War were fitted with blue Yankee uniforms, given rifles and marched right back to the plantations and deltas they had left, to burn and kill those who had committed crimes against their race. They were promised "40 acres and a mule," which became a mantra of freedom from slavery. It was an empty promise. I'm still waiting for mine.

When the slaves were freed and the Civil War was declared over, there was at first a flourishing of Negro culture in America — our race thrived in the arts, in government and as property owners. Black faces were seen, and voices heard in high places. The beginnings of dignity were being established.

But the economic reality of the need for cheap, hard-working labor created a power structure throughout the South that was as effective as any slave market. Sharecropping gave the appearance of fairness but left Negroes powerless and enslaved – with bonds that were just as unbreakable as heavy steel chains. It worked like this:

The landowner owned the land, and provided the mules, plows, fatback, corn and syrup. At the General Store, the sharecropper had to have a credit ledger. If you did not have credit, you could not eat. Whatever crops you grew or product you produced were strictly accounted for and at the end of the year, when the crops were collected, was "settlin' time." For every bushel of corn, the landowner got two and the sharecropper got one. For cotton, two bales went to the landowner and one went to the sharecropper. The math was simple: The sharecropper was always in debt – with no way out. When the sharecropper went to "settle" with the General Store, the plantation owner would pull out his ledger and tell you what you owed. When he lied and cheated in the accounting, there was nothing you could do about it.

Later in life I worked at such a store in Montgomery as a stock boy. The owner was illiterate, so he would hire a hillbilly white boy to come down from the mountains and run the cash register. The white boy had a third grade education. I was taking advanced calculus and analytical geometry in high school, but was not considered capable of working the cash register. I lifted boxes and emptied the trash.

My father, Will, was a hard-working man who could neither read nor write. He couldn't even write his name. He fathered 13 children, 11 of whom survived. I was the third child. We were all delivered by a midwife, my great aunt Della. Because of the lack of record keeping and education, most of us have had a difficult time obtaining our birth certificates.

My father was not a field-worker, however. He tended the garden of the plantation owner, Mr. Farrior, and ran the dairy of more than 200 cows. He supervised the milking and the milk processing and was paid about $12 a month. I never knew him to make more than $80 a month, and that was long after I was away from home.

Dad had worked for this family all his life, since he was about seven years old, when he was a little "house boy." Each generation had kept him on. He was a fearful man – never aggressive toward whites. The Farriors trusted him.

Mother worked inside the house as well, washing and ironing. She took in laundry for other families and earned $1.50 per week. She, too, was trusted, and we grew up thinking we were privileged, and being treated as privileged, because we were allowed to interact regularly with whites. We had a slightly higher status than the 242 other sharecroppers who worked the plantation. Imagine 242 people working for pitiful wages! Mr. Farrior was amassing great wealth by this system, just as the landowners had before him.

Our house was like every other sharecropper house in ramshackle row. It was a shotgun house – front door facing the back door. Two rooms and a back porch, an outhouse and a well. All the houses looked alike. Our five boys slept on the back porch. We were closer in experience to our African ancestors, who slept under the sky, than we were to our white neighbors. It was deplorable.

My mother, Amanda, had a very solid African background, but my father had very prominent American Indian features. His mother was mostly full-blooded American Indian. She loved to have me brush her long, straight hair. My granddaddy, John Smith, was outspoken against injustice. When he heard that a black person had been beaten, you had to tie him down so he wouldn't go on a rampage. "He's crazy," my grandmother would say. In the South, if you spoke up for justice, you were a fool. But granddaddy spoke. Whites thought he was crazy and kept their distance.

The Farriors had three children who were taught to treat Negroes with some decency. The oldest son, Dixon, had a kind disposition like his father. Next was a daughter, Anne, and the youngest child was John. I was about five years younger than John, and he changed the course of my life.

I believe that God has been the designer and mover of circumstances throughout my entire life. Just as He spared Moses from slavery, I feel that I was spared from the deprivation most Southern blacks experienced. You remember the story from the book of Exodus. The Jews were slaves in Egypt, with increasing injustice and hatred around them. The Pharaoh ordered that all male Jewish babies be slain when Moses was a few months old. His mother lovingly made a basket of bulrushes and tar, laid him inside and set it on the riverbank. Miriam, his older sister, was nearby keeping watch.

The Princess and her entourage went to the river to bathe, and there she found the baby Moses in his hiding place. She lifted him from the basket and God softened her heart to rescue him. As she prepared to take the baby back to the palace, Miriam stepped forward. "I know a woman who can nurse the baby for you," she offered. So Moses' mother was reunited with him and nursed him. Instead of being murdered, Moses grew up in the palace, where he was trained and educated. God chose him for the future leadership of his people.

Now, the nature of the palace didn't change. Pharaoh was still a murderer. Hatred and prejudice were still rampant. But, like most hate, it did not apply to the individual in their midst. Moses was part of Pharaoh's family and that gave him tremendous privileges.

When I heard the story of Moses, I began to think of my-self as "Little Black Moses" because in the same way that God directed the life of Moses, He directed my life. I, too, was plucked from the anonymity of my community to a special place of recognition. I became the playmate of John Farrior. I be-came his "colored boy."

In essence I was invited into the "palace." The plantation was open to me when I was by John's side. And I was privileged. When the Farriors bought John a pony, they bought me a pony. When John had a special treat, I had a special treat. When they went into Montgomery to buy clothes for John, they bought clothes for me, which I wore proudly. But, of course, prejudice hovered closely over the privileges.

"Don't you ever let me catch any one of your little brothers wearing any of these clothes that I buy for you," Mrs. Farrior warned me. Even at a young age I saw the wrongness in that. I resented it, but there was nothing I could do about it. We made sure she never caught us.

Still, in that era, as the South struggled out of the Depression, I became visible to the community at large. As John's "boy," I was able to interact with the extended world in a way denied other Negroes. And we had fun. The two of us would ride our horses and shoot down fences with rifles. We operated the plantation store and sold goods to the neighbors.

One time John was fooling around and accidentally set fire to a field. He took all of those fighting the fire down to our store and gave them cigarettes and made them swear not to tell his daddy. At a time when my brothers and sisters would gather little bits of copper or iron from the side of the road to get a little money, I was selling items from a counter and taking care of a shop. The fact that none of it was mine had not yet mattered. It felt like mine. I was treated as special and I felt I was special. That feeling never went away.

At the age of eight or nine I took care of Mrs. Farrior's 200 chickens every morning and every evening during the six months that I was able to attend school each year. Every once in a while, when we would get very hungry at home, I would "lose" one of the chickens. I thought I was clever, but, of course, everyone knew what had happened. Still, it felt good to watch my mother's hands plucking the feathers, rubbing salt into the skin and serving the chicken to my brothers and sisters.

When I was 13, I was the brightest child in school. I had be-come a milker in the dairy, getting up at dawn to labor with my father. I had dreams of my future, hoping to become a doctor or a great scientist, but as each year unfolded I understood more fully the injustices that made up reality in Lowndes County, Alabama, the most bigoted county in the history of the nation. Only $39 a year per student was spent on education in schools for black children. School was in session only a few months a year for Negroes. Not one of my teachers had graduated from college. I had no money. How could I get more education?

One strong cultural aspect of our lives was church. In Sunday school I would listen to the stories of faith and liberation. Oppression was not something that started in 1619, when slavery was instituted in this country. We black sharecroppers could equate our situation with the old Bible stories describing how people who were oppressed reacted to their oppression. I always identified with my Hebrew brothers and sisters who, in many areas and many ways, have had to struggle.

Some of our religious leaders spoke openly of our oppression. Dr. Vernon Johns was pastor of the Dexter Avenue Baptist Church in Montgomery before young Martin Luther King Jr. was called to that pulpit. He preached a sermon that was famous throughout the South.

"Racial justice in Alabama?" he bellowed from the platform. "There is none! A black person's life is not worth that of a rabbit.

Why? Because there are only certain months of the year when you can kill a rabbit. A Negro can be killed anytime."

* * *

So, on that dusty, hot day, as Henry and I went off to the General Store with our list, I was happy. Like most young Negro boys, I always carried a "walking stick," and I swung mystick along during the two-mile walk to town.

But then, coming toward me on the sidewalk was a group of white boys. Encountering whites on the sidewalk was always tense. Anything could happen. The Negro was supposed to get off the sidewalk and walk in the street when a white came from the other direction. One of the boys coming toward me was a big kid, and a bully, plain and simple. He disrespected blacks and harassed them, hit them, spit on them and stole from them – all normal for a white boy in that era. As they got closer, my resolve solidified. I kept walking on the sidewalk.

"Hey, nigger! Get out of the way!" he called out. My brother Henry jumped into the street, terrified. I kept my ground as they got closer. I could smell their anger, but I kept my ground. When we got close enough to touch, they pushed me – but I pushed back and whacked that white boy with my walking stick until he was set on his ass on the sidewalk of Hayneville, Alabama. Henry

23

ran the two miles home.

I kept on walking and went into the store and read from my list. No one would dare retaliate because my father belonged to the Farriors, my mother worked in their house, and I was John Farrior's "colored boy." I had the protection of the palace.

George Walker Smith, Knoxville College, 1948

Section One
Little Black Moses

Chapter Two
Klling the Egyptian

At the end of the ninth grade, I was at the head of my class and eager for learning. But there was no high school for Negroes. Lowndes County would not spend any hard-won taxpayer money on educating blacks, who were supposed to be serving whites with menial labor. The mentality at the time was to keep the Negro community ignorant, illiterate and oppressed. They wouldn't spend a dime to better a young black student. But God had a plan.

One Saturday afternoon, I was milking cows along with my father when Mr. Farrior called for us to come up to his house. We stood on the porch and then this plantation owner did something unheard of in our county.

"Will," he said, "George is too damn smart not to continue in school. Down in Wilcox County there are some schools for Negroes. I want you to go see Knight tomorrow and tell him that I said to get George into school."

We were stunned. It was very unusual and extraordinary for a plantation owner to give up the hard work of a strong back in order to permit a sharecropper's son to be educated.

Mr. Knight was a farm agent who worked with the black sharecroppers to upgrade farming practices and he traveled throughout the lower South. What he had discovered was that back in the 1800s, the Presbyterian Church had dedicated its resources to providing schools for Negroes. There were 245 Presbyterian schools, from elementary through graduate seminary, available for black students in the Southern states. The school in Wilcox County had been given to the church by a homesteader from Ohio who was Presbyterian.

So, one Sunday, in the later part of August, my father and I went with Mr. Knight in his car away from Hayneville, leaving Lowndes County behind us. I didn't really believe that I would be able to go. Something would go wrong, something would happen that would send our car back to our gravel road, our shotgun house. I would unpack the little cardboard box that held my belongings and in the morning I would get up at dawn and milk cows. But that's not what happened.

We came to Wilcox County Training School and I saw expanses of grass, a neatly kept farm and garden, and rows of school buildings. Faster than I could imagine, I was being introduced to administrators, and then to other students. And then came the goodbyes.

My father shook my hand and looked away. He didn't fully understand the importance of education and would have rather had me help out with the cows.

Mother was the spark that kept my love of learning aflame.

She was a brilliant woman. If she had had more advantages and education, she would have been a Harriet Tubman or a Mary McCloud Bethune or a Barbara Jordan. I got my love of learning and my persistence from my mother, and she never failed to support my aspirations.

Here was a woman who, for most of my young life, had been pregnant. She worked hard interacting on a daily basis with the prejudices of the white society while earning less than two dollars a week, at the same time struggling against the difficulties of feeding and clothing 11 children. Even so, she always had enough to share with others in need. She always gave to everyone else, even when she had nothing.

Mother had seen the benefit of the activities and the education that I was seeking and supported me in every way she could. If it had not been for her, I would have been doomed to a life a physical labor.

My mother was also one of the most deeply spiritual folks that I knew and provided the whole family with spiritual guidance. She lived out her religion and could see straight through hypocrisy. Every Sunday morning we would be off at 6 a.m. in an assembly line, taking baths in the tub and dressing in the best rags that we owned. Once we were ready, Dad would make sure that he walked all of us children in a line behind him from home to church for Sunday school. He did that faithfully, even though he himself did not attend the service.

Dad didn't really think about his own relationship with God until all of us were grown, but he supported my mother in what she tried to do for the church. Even with his limited education and limited understanding of spirituality, Dad realized the importance of spiritual matters in the life of his kids.

Once we were grown and gone, I was told that Dad had started attending church sometimes and was sort of getting into the groove. Then one Sunday, he was sitting down near the front when the minister jumped up on the platform and said, "And now we'll be led in prayer by Brother Smith!"

He got down on his knees and crawled right out the door. The next time Brother Smith went back to that church was in his casket!

One of my greatest joys in life came when I went back to Hayneville and bought my parents an acre of land. They had never owned an inch of land in their lives. It was the happiest day my mother ever experienced. Dad died before I could put the triple-wide mobile home on the land, but it was a joy to be able to give that home to my dear mother. None of it would have happened without the opportunity that I had been given to attend Wilcox

County Training School.

After I said goodbye to Dad, I went to my room and lay on the bed, looking out the window. It was the first night in my life that I had a bed to myself. The dormitory was clean, and there was running water and a toilet. I had never felt so hopeful.

My three years in high school were glorious. I was overcome with the amount of learning that was available to the hard-working student and was broadened by the experiences of young blacks from outside Alabama. I discovered the challenges and satisfaction of organized sports. Mathematics and science continued to be my strongest subjects and I dreamed still of medical school and a career as a physician.

During the summer, I worked on the school farm. I never had a dime to put toward my education, so it felt good to be contributing to the upkeep and support of the school, knowing that a basket of corn would be worth a basket of corn, and a bucket of beans would be worth a bucket of beans. The administrators and teachers appreciated my skill and intelligence, which made the tasks welcome. I still didn't have a cent to my name and it wasn't until college that I was able to earn actual money. Toward the end of my last high school term, Mother got word that I was to be Valedictorian of the senior class.

The graduation ceremony was victorious. I wore a suit for the first time in my life, one that had been sent down from white churches in the north. Being Valedictorian was an amazing achievement for someone from Lowndes County, Alabama, and I made many in my family and community very proud. Who would believe that George Walker Smith had graduated from high school, and was the head of his class?

My speech was full of hope. I spoke of opportunity, of equality, of blessing. After the ceremony, two white women from the Presbyterian Church in Pittsburgh made their way to my circle of family members. Each year these women would come to the graduation since their church gave financial support to the school. Mrs. Shear and Mrs. Voorhes were active in the church and their husbands taught at the theological seminary in Pittsburgh. Mr. Shear taught homiletics and Mr. Voorhes was the business manager of the seminary.

"George, we're going to be praying that you come to seminary in Pittsburgh," one of them said. "We think that you would be a wonderful preacher."

Preaching was the last thing on my mind. No way! I wanted to make money, not starve! I had hoped to go to college and then become a doctor. Of course Negroes weren't allowed to attend college in Alabama, let alone medical school. But I had never seen a black doctor and thought I would like to become one. I opened my Valedictorian scholarship envelope and the last spark of hope of becoming a doctor quietly died. It contained $100.

But this is where the faith of many people became a part of my life. At the time there were teachers, administrators, family members and two unknown white ladies praying for George Smith. Good white folk and good black folk who saw some potential and stood by me. They urged me to go to the Presbyterian college for Negroes in Knoxville, Tennessee. Knoxville College had been established by the Presbyterian Church in 1865 for the education of Negroes. I enrolled with great anticipation.

Dad was disappointed in me. He needed help at the dairy of the plantation and on the farm. He didn't understand that I wanted more from life than to live with the injustices that he absorbed daily. But there was no going backward for me. In fact, there never has been. Setbacks, yes, but no facing backward. That I have not done.

I stayed with my uncle in Montgomery to work so that I could have a change of underwear and a new pair of shoes for school. In August, new students were called to Knoxville College for an orientation. I arrived at the Registrars office with my $100 and not a dime more. I had no idea how it would work out.

That first day, a few of us freshmen got together and were dribbling a basketball, headed for the gym. A white man was coming from that direction and met us with a smile. He greeted us and introduced himself as Mr. Frazier, the business manager of the school.

"I'm George Smith," I said, shaking his hand.

"Oh, yes!" he said, "From Miller's Ferry, the Wilcox School, is that right?"

"Yes, I am," I said and started to turn away. Then I turned back and said, "Mr. Frazier, thank you for the scholarship that you gave me."

"Well, you're welcome, George," he said.

For the next four years, I had no idea how I was going to pay for anything at school. Others who couldn't pay their bills were sent home. But the business manager, a white Virginian, never called me in to discuss my account. I was never asked to pay.

I did, however, work hard. I had three jobs on campus and each was more wonderful than the last. At Knoxville College there was a tall belfry and I was the official bell ringer for everything that happened meals, chapel, classes and other events. I loved to ring those mighty bells. It also gave me a little bit of status with the other students, who called me "Dude."

"Dude, can you get us out five minutes early?" some girls would ask.

"I'll do it for a little kiss."

The dean would catch up with me later in the day and say, "Mr. Smith, your watch must be wrong."

I would look back at him and then look down at my watch.

"Hey, Dean Cherry, you must be right."

My second job was working in the library, which was like throwing a fox into a chicken house. In addition to satisfying my love of books, it satisfied my need to flirt a little. There were a lot of good-looking girls in the library.

My third job was working in the cafeteria, so, of course, I was able to eat. But more importantly, I was able to sneak food to my dorm mates.

"Hey, Dude! Can you get us some food tonight?"

It may have been nothing more than eggs and bacon, but I would wrap it up and toss it over the wall, where my dorm mates would be waiting to catch it.

Attending Knoxville College was, again, a time of listening, learning and leadership. I was becoming educated in the history of injustice against blacks and learned that I could hate injustice without color boundaries. Seeing injustice against whites riled me also. I chaffed against a society that upheld the status quo, when the status quo was based on unjust power structures. But I was also finding pockets of justice, niches of equality.

Here, for the first time, I met white people who did not treat me with disdain. There were white professors who applauded me as they challenged me. Whites who treated me with some decency and threw their arms around me because they saw the potential that I had. This was a phenomenon to me. I attributed it more to their education than to their faith. But I began to see that not every white person was my oppressor.

There was one professor, Dr. William Ruderman, a German with two Ph.D. degrees: one from the University of Heidelberg and one from the University of Hamburg. For some reason, he took a liking to me and I respected him so much that I minored in German. I was president of the German Club, even though my major subject was chemistry and I had a second minor in biology. After I graduated, Dr. Ruderman would send me a book each year – one he considered the best philosophy book published that year.

Not everyone was as unbiased as my friend the German professor.

It was during one summer of my college years that I worked in a Montgomery, Alabama, grocery store as a box boy. It was a typical Southern store in those days – warm and humid, with barrels of plump green pickles, and bins of flour, grain, tobacco. Boxed and canned items lined some shelves and even some glass jars of hard candy sat on the counter by the cash box.

One hot afternoon two white couples came in, uniformed captains in the army and their wives. They got a nod from the store owner's wife, and I watched as one captain walked over to the segregated drinking fountain and pointed to the label.

"Look!" he said, "Colored water!" He bent over to take a drink. "I've never seen colored water coming from a drinking fountain before, have you?" He let the water splash into his puckered lips, then stood up and put his hat back on. "Tastes just like regular water to me!"

I had to turn around to keep from laughing.

"That water's for the niggers," muttered the owner.

The wives twittered with giggles and the foursome paid for their items and left. It was one of the first times I had seen defiance of injustice in a white man.

All across the South, however, the winds of the civil rights movement were beginning to stir and the rigid structure of desegregation was showing cracks and fissures. World War II had seen the desegregation of the armed services and in 1950 there was an expectation that the equality of combat would be carried over into hometowns and cities across America. We didn't yet realize that the expectation would end in disappointment.

At college I was a success – a popular basketball player, an exemplary student and a good dancer. I had discovered the joys of being in the company of young ladies and found that I had a natural charisma that charmed them. So, it was with some surprise that I asked a certain Irene Hightower for a date and she turned me down flat. She was the first young lady who had turned me down.

Irene was from the town of Nicholasville, Kentucky. At six years old, she was the oldest of three children when her mother died. Her father vowed not to re-marry until the children were out of high school, so Irene grew into the role of motherhood very early. She is still a wonderfully maternal woman. This, and her tremendous strength of character, is what attracted me to her. She was two years ahead of me at college, having had to interrupt her education to work, and had now returned to finish school. She was not the most beautiful or the most loveable woman – she was the most wonderful.

If I asked Irene to a concert, she would not go. She did not believe in going to concerts, so I gave the tickets away. She expected the best of me and let me know if I did not live up to that expectation. She has let me know, if fact, nearly every day for over 50 years.

As my college years ended, I was again near the head of my class. On the day of graduation, my fraternity brothers and I were serenading in a circle, singing farewell songs to the campus. Mr. Frazier came over with that same grin on his face. He shook my hand and hugged me.

"Thank you, Mr. Frazier," I suddenly had to say. "Thank you for all you did for me over these four years. I wasn't always an angel. In fact, I always wanted to be in on the action, good or bad. Why were you so good to me?"

"Well, George," he said, "remember the first day you came to this campus and you were on the way to the gym? I remembered that when I introduced myself, you thanked me for the $100 scholarship. Do you know that that year I gave out 286 scholarships? Only you and one other cared enough to thank me for it."

I have always said that I got through college on two words – Thank You.

None of us makes it on our own, no matter how brilliant or wealthy. We all need to be in a position where we can say thank you. Never have an ungrateful heart or you may miss out on incredible blessings.

I had come to Knoxville College as a young, inexperienced and naïve black student. I was leaving a confident, 21-year-old scholar, with a wonderful woman by my side. Irene and I had scrapped together the $1.25 for a wedding license.

On July 4, Irene sent me out with my friends to have my last wild, Independence Day celebration.

"Have fun tonight, because tomorrow we're getting married and independence is over," called out Irene.

The next day, July 5, 1951, we were married. As Irene and I were walking away from the church, I noticed that they had marked on the license that she was a white woman. I immediately went back.

"Reverend Dumas, you tell them that I did not marry a white woman. I married a colored woman."

I was not about to be lynched in Alabama over a clerical error.

After the excitement of our wedding was over, I felt utterly lost.

Being back in Alabama was oppressive. During the summer I

went to Alabama State University to study for a master's degree in Education. In the fall I started a position as a teacher and found I was fighting ignorance and a negative mind-set as much as a lack of knowledge.

The hope for equality that was raised during the war years was quickly deteriorating. As black soldiers returned home from overseas, Southern society slammed the door on their respect and pride. Jobs were not open to them and training was not valued. The freedom that so many had fought for did not belong to them. They had laid their lives on the line for white America, as it turned out, and white America did not respect the sacrifice. During the war, thousands of black soldiers had been to Europe, Africa and the Pacific where they were not discriminated against. They had tasted equality and it made home more bitter than ever.

The Bible tells us in the book of Exodus that Moses grew up in the palace of the Pharaoh and was given a meticulous education. Other historians of the period, Josephus and Philo, describe this education in detail. He had access to the great writings of ancient wisdom. He was trained in philosophy, logic and political thought. Moses had also been trained physically and possessed strength and confidence. His education had removed prejudice and inequality from his behavior.

There came a time when Moses decided to discover his roots. He went to see his countrymen, and what he saw appalled him. The Hebrews were enslaved and starving. They had cruel and indecent taskmasters who mocked their plight and practiced injustice for sport. The young man was trying to absorb this when he witnessed an Egyptian beating his Hebrew slave. The injustice overcame him.

Moses looked around. No one was in sight. His rage vented and he killed the Egyptian. The slave ran off and Moses hastily dug a shallow grave in the sand and covered up his misdeed. The young man was educated but naïve.

The next day he went back to the area and saw a Hebrew man striking another Hebrew. He said to the man who had hit the other, "Why are you hitting your own countryman?"

"Who made you a prince?" the belligerent man answered. "Who made you the judge? Are you going to kill me the way you killed the Egyptian?"

So Moses knew that the murder had been found out and fled. He went to an isolated part of Egypt where nomads roamed and sat down near a community well. In a while he saw seven women, daughters of the priest of Midian, coming to draw water for their sheep. But the mountain men, the shepherds, would not let the women near the well and tried to drive them away. Moses' ire was again raised against injustice. He defended the women and watered their sheep for them. By this act of justice, Moses was rewarded. He was brought to the home of the priest where he was treated with honor, and given a feast. He shortly married one of the daughters and became absorbed into the family of the priest of Midian.

Like Moses, I had been educated enough to become enraged at any injustice around me. All the rationales for hatred, prejudice, arrogance and cruelty do not stand up when a mind has been educated and trained to discern truth. The dissonance inside of me was growing each day in that humid climate – that rich, fertile soil of Alabama.

I was not trained in nonviolence. Once someone hit Martin Luther King Jr. over the head with a Bible. If it had happened to me, I would have hit that man over the head with a chair. Since the time as an eight-year-old when I knocked that white bully on his backside, I have responded forcefully to any physical threat. It was not my nature to sit back. As the oppression of blacks became more frequently tinged with violence, I became increasingly tense.

Two things happened that drove me away from Alabama for good.

It was settlin' time just after the spring harvest. A young woman who was seven months pregnant went to the General Store in the town where I was teaching to settle her account.

"This is what you bought and this is what you owe," said the landowner.

"But I didn't buy that," said the woman.

"That's what the book says."

"I never got that," she said.

"You gotta pay what the book says," insisted the man.

"The book is wrong," she said.

Without another word, he pulled out a .45 and shot her through the stomach. Murder plain as day. He ordered the blacks to carry her body out of the store and clean up the blood. Nothing at all happened to that man. The sheriff did not even come to investigate. I was boiling mad.

About three weeks later, another incident occurred. Tucked away from the farmland, back along some riverbeds or in isolated areas, there were pockets of black families who owned land in Alabama. Some were inheritances left over from the Reconstruction era, some had been able to accumulate some money and buy unwanted land, some were squatters who had been driven off their plantations by whites. These landowning blacks had been forced into self-sufficiency and were a sort of underground economy. Often these people would make moonshine liquor and set up little dance halls where blacks could go to find entertainment, let off a little steam, drink, dance, listen to music and enjoy one another.

In the neighborhood where I was teaching, there was a woman who had had several strokes and couldn't speak. Her family hosted these little socials at her house along the Alabama River to raise money for her.

One cool Saturday night, there was a crowd at the mute woman's house. Lights from the house danced along the river and reflected the starry sky. People were relaxing. Fish sandwiches, hot dogs, pickles and other food was aplenty. Music was playing and they were selling a little moonshine.

Without warning, the local sheriff and his deputy and the Alabama Highway Patrol came out to raid the party and break it up. Now, what the Highway Patrol was doing there I'll never know. It was far away from any interstate. But white authority came in force. Everyone started to clear out.

The mute woman who owned the house was sitting in the corner and a Highway Patrolman noticed her and said to her, "Now, what the hell is an old lady like you doing up so late at night?"

45

Of course, she couldn't answer. The room was deathly still.

"Are you gonna answer me?"

He took out his blackjack and swung it into her head. The blow knocked her off the chair and her bleeding body stretched across the floor. She died on that floor, as the sheriff looked on. Those white dogs turned and drove off into the night.

The next morning my rage overflowed. I caught it on paper. I sat down and wrote a lengthy indictment against the injustice in Alabama, the white murderers that lived in our midst, the sins of segregation and kept writing until I had articulated all of my indignation at inequality. It was superb. And it was lethal.

Folding the paper carefully and putting it into an envelope, I dressed with resolve and set out for the post office. The letter was addressed to the *Montgomery Advertiser*, the major newspaper of the region that had a circulation encompassing nearly the entire state. My plan was to speak up against the wrongs of Alabama. I knew that the newspaper would surely print the letter and that it would very likely cost my life, but I was willing to lay down my life for justice. God had a different plan.

On the way to the post office, I ran into the principal of the school where I was now vice principal. He stopped to greet me and I let him read the letter. What happened next shocked me.

He literally got on his knees beside me and pleaded.

"George," he begged, "don't do this! The Ku Klux Klan will come into this town and kill all of the Negroes! Every one of us will be murdered — our children and our wives. Please don't do this to us!"

I looked down into his face. His ardent pleading helped me understand both my power and my helplessness. He was right. In a racist society like Alabama, the forcefulness of sheer truth would bring evil retaliation to innocent people.

We sat and hung our heads.

"KP," I said, "I've got to leave Alabama."

I knew that my tolerance for injustice was reaching critical mass. I knew that the next time I witnessed injustice I would, like Moses, take matters to a violent end. I had to flee.

I finished the last few months of the school year and went again up to Montgomery State for the summer. We didn't talk much about the situation, but both Irene and I knew that a change was needed. Some time during that hot summer we sat on the porch of our house and talked about the future.

"George," Irene said, "you want to go to that seminary in Pittsburgh, don't you?"

I looked at her sweet face, so faithful to me and so

understanding. I thought about those two white women at my graduation who were praying for me and wondered at the power of prayer and the providence of God. It wasn't really my decision; it was God's leading. He would deal with the state of Alabama in His way and in His time, but I would be far away by then.

"I think I do."

We wrote to the seminary and things fell in line surprisingly easily. By summer's end, we had packed our belongings, said our farewells and started the journey north to Pittsburgh. This time I had a suitcase.

In the Bible, in the book of Luke, it says that Jesus sent his disciples out to proclaim the Kingdom of God. He told them to teach and heal those who would accept the message.

"As for those who do not welcome you," Jesus said, "when you leave their town, shake the dust from your feet."

We left Alabama shaking off the dust of hatred, segregation, injustice and inequality.

Mrs. C. O. Vance helped George go to College

Section One
Little Black Moses

Chapter Three
The Promised Land

The crux of the Christian religion is the belief in a God who takes a personal interest in all that He has created. He takes a personal interest in you. He takes a personal interest in me. Never was this more clearly understood by me than when Irene and I arrived in Pittsburgh, Pennsylvania.

The first blessing was finding that the little apartment the seminary had found for us was furnished. This was unexpected! The student who had lived there before us had gone to Pakistan and left his furniture. We ran from room to room, overjoyed that there was a bed, chairs and a table. And a desk. Now, some of our meager savings could go toward books and other necessities. Next, Irene was able to find a job without difficulty. She worked in the literature department of United Presbyterian Women. This was a necessity for a seminary wife not just for financial reasons, but to ward off sheer loneliness. Seminary education is hell.

Theological seminary trains bright young men and women in the doctrines of the church, of course, and techniques of preaching. Most importantly, however, it creates biblical scholars who can plumb the depths of the mysteries of God. Students must learn Greek and Hebrew, the original languages of the biblical documents. Students must learn the rules that define

51

biblical scholarship in interpreting the Scriptures. They learn the historical context in which the Bible's chapters were written, and about the history and context of each writer to better understand the wording and the meaning.

In addition, seminary teaches the history of the church – the long traditions that have stretched without interruption from the itinerant preaching missions of Jesus' followers to the great European congregations in massive cathedrals and to the Vatican itself. Church history teaches how the radical news of Christ's birth and death and resurrection was a holy sacrifice for all of creation. How has this news been told and how has the message been spread to the rest of the world? What creeds were written to summarize the Gospel and codify the belief system? What happened when Martin Luther left the Catholic priesthood and declared that the Catholic religion was not representing biblical Christianity? How did the great denominations come about and what is the difference between them, anyway?

Finally, theological seminary forces you to tackle the great mysteries of the faith, beyond the obvious – miracles and the virgin birth. How can the trinity be explained? How did God become incarnate in Jesus Christ and what does it mean to us? Are we called by the Holy Spirit to salvation or predisposed? Are all called?

What, exactly, is salvation?

At any good theological seminary, you will learn the answers to these questions. At a great seminary, you will be asked the questions and will have to find your own answers. Pittsburgh Theological Seminary was an excellent one.

In addition to the academic life at seminary, there is a requirement that each first-year student be assigned a practicum at a church, where you get actual experience in doing ministry. Dr. Shear was in charge of assigning students to their internships. There were only two black Presbyterian churches in Pittsburgh. Virgil, who was a light-skinned Negro, was placed in a middle-class Negro church not too far from the seminary without much of a problem. The other black church was a poor ghetto church that was barely alive. Dr. Shear decided that he would no longer limit the black students to serving in black churches. "They are Presbyterians like everybody else," he said.

The school administrators were a little frantic wondering where they would find a church that could accept me as an intern. Then they talked to Howard Jamieson, the pastor of Third Presbyterian Church in Squirrel Hill.

"We absolutely will hire George," said the pastor. "It's a one-year commitment, right?" He took the matter to his church session.

Out of 36 members, all but one voted in my favor. God was going to teach me one of the most profound lessons of my life. And He was going to teach Squirrel Hill a thing or two at the same time.

Squirrel Hill is a historic area of beautiful, graceful homes near the University of Pittsburgh, owned by beautiful, graceful people. White people. Rich people. There were CEOs of great industries, high-ranking state officials, and old-moneyed gentlemen of leisure.

The church itself was large and stately. It was made of gray stone with gothic architecture. It was surrounded by lawns, trees – a beautiful setting. In an effort to attract youth, a bowling alley was installed in the basement of the church. When the church needed to replace the carpeting in the sanctuary, the bill came to $75,000. This congregation had lots of money.

It was here that I learned that good people come in all colors, a lesson I will take to my grave.

I began working with the youth, leading their programs and caring about them individually. I taught them that God does not see color, but looks at the heart. I explained that to be a follower of Jesus, they had to come to Him without their riches, prejudices or status and bow at His feet. And He would lift them up and love them alone for who they were, not what they had. Then I taught them to care for one another. As God changed these young people, we came to love each other. At the end of the year, they insisted that I stay another year, and then another. I served all three years of seminary at the church.

Meanwhile, the message against pride and separation caught the attention of the community. I had found my weapon against injustice and was wielding it effectively.

It was about this time that Emmett Till was killed, and it got the attention of the nation.

Emmett was a young black teenager who had gone down from Chicago to visit his cousins in the South. He was not "trained" in the humility that was necessary for survival. The two young cousins went into the General Store and a white lady was behind the counter. She accused him of winking at her. Who knows what actually happened. That night the whites came to get him; his body was found in the river the next morning.

Many churches in America were shaken by this event and groups invited me to speak out on the topic of "Brotherly Love." It was an opportunity to start folks thinking about injustice. Soon afterward, three young boys – two Jewish boys and a black boy – were killed in Mississippi. It started people wanting to re-examine their philosophies. When there was a protest march in the South, the police commissioner turned water hoses and dogs on the human beings who were seeking justice, treating them like rats in Harlem.

These despicable events gave me the opportunity to address racial injustice to rich white folks in Pittsburgh.

I began to have a white friend organize my time and book my speaking engagements. At one point, he had about 130 talks lined up. Dr. Addison Leach, my favorite professor at the seminary, would tell the class, "George has caused a revolution in Pittsburgh, one for the better. Those folks over there love him and Irene and Tony."

Once, at a service club in Aliquippa, the president of Alcoa was there. After I spoke, he came up to me.

"George," he said, "if I could find 100 Negroes like you, I would personally send them across this nation to speak as you have spoken to us white folks here tonight."

But in the '50s in America, there were only a handful of my race like me. America didn't want black leaders. The first leadership opportunities were only available because the institutions of our democracy were forced by legislation to provide them – the military, organized sports and entertainment. The church was actually not on the list. At my own seminary there were some students who questioned whether Virgil and I could "make it" academically when we first arrived. I ended up tutoring some of those same students in Hebrew until 2 and 3 in the morning. Of all the stupid injustices, the one that makes me the most angry is the idea that the color of my skin has anything to do with the capacity of my intellect. That is plain dumb.

But other institutions were more readily integrated. The desegregation of the military allowed for training and distinction regardless of color. Of course there was prejudice and injustice experienced by individual soldiers, but military desegregation codified the American stand on equality for people of all races.

In sports, the impact of Jackie Robinson in integrating baseball can never be fully appreciated. It changed everything for black athletes. In entertainment, Billie Holiday, Louis Armstrong, Charlie Parker and Nat King Cole were creating integrated audiences and gathering the economic forces that would allow black-owned Motown Records to dominate the record charts in the '60s. Where the dollar is almighty, people change their behavior and segregation is forgotten. Where the Almighty is almighty, people change their hearts and segregation is forgotten. In America, it is much easier to change people's behavior than it is to change their hearts.

But hearts were changing, one at a time, in Pittsburgh, Pennsylvania.

For Irene and me and our little son Tony, one of the exciting parts of being in this church was the opportunity to house-sit. Every so often a family would be taking a trip and would ask us to stay at their home. Jim and Mary Anne Ludwig, who, with his father, owned the largest florist business in Pittsburgh, asked us once. They planned a trip to Europe for the summer and asked us to stay at their lovely home in Fox Chapel. If you know the area, you know that Fox Chapel is very, very exclusive – one of the first upper-class suburbs in America.

We listened carefully as they explained the details about caring for the house. "We left lots of food in the freezer, so help yourselves," they said.

When they left us alone, we went through the house, marveling at their beautiful furniture and well-appointed rooms. Then we went into the kitchen and looked into the freezer. It was packed with food. "Lamb" said one label. We had never tasted lamb! In the South you ate either pork or goat. Irene made a meal out of that lamb that I will never forget. So much for being a "starving" preacher!

The generosity and apparent lack of disdain toward the color of our skin was impressive to us. It gave us hope. Back in Alabama we weren't allowed in restaurants with whites and here we were, eating off their plates and using their silverware. So, it was a joyous summer of liberation from hatred for Irene and me.

Years later – more than 50 years later – Jim and Mary Anne came to visit Irene and me in San Diego, and I learned the truth about that summer. It seems that the two neighbors on either side of Jim's house had formed a conspiracy. One of them even called himself a "born-again" Christian. They had planned to burn down the house while we were inside, so disturbed they were to have "niggers" in their midst. Somehow God stayed their hands and we were allowed to enjoy the lack of prejudice that our host and hostess had shown to us. There are good and bad people of any color.

Sooner than we had imagined it was time to leave Pittsburgh. I had been assigned to go to San Diego, a sleepy beach town dominated by military bases and retired military personnel. Third Presbyterian Church in Pittsburgh insisted on hosting my ordination and the service was packed. The daughter of the one session member who had voted against my internship asked me if she could sing. She sang "Walk Worthy." It was an amazing turnaround.

Irene and I were in for another surprise. The church had taken a collection and handed over the keys to a brand new, light green 1956 Ford! We were thrilled! It was the most enjoyable car I ever drove, because it didn't cost me a dime. They had enough collected to also give us $5,000, which was a fortune in those days. Irene and I packed little Tony and our belongings and said tearful goodbyes to the kids, the pastors, the professors and our friends.

Dr. Leach had often said, "They love you, George, at that church. But would they feel the same if you brought fifty of your Negro friends to church every Sunday?"

It was the right question to ask. I was going to organize a church in San Diego where the neighborhood was experiencing "white flight." The white congregation was moving out to the suburbs to a new church and the Presbytery was bringing in a black pastor. Not everyone was happy about that, as I would soon discover.

As Irene and I drove across country, first we drove through Kentucky to see her family, then on to Knoxville to see friends at the college. Finally, we stopped in to visit my family in Hayneville, Alabama. Mrs. Farrior, who was now a widow, ran out of the house and embraced me. One of the Negroes was startled and ran like lightning to warn my mother, "Amanda! Amanda! There's a white woman up there hugging George!"

"I was the one who got you your education, you know," Mrs. Farrior kept repeating. It was completely untrue. She may have

60

given me moral support over the years, but there was never any monetary support. Still, I felt sorry for her. Her oldest son had died young. Her daughter had married a Buick dealer and moved away. John had been expelled from school for taking alcohol on campus.

The Bible tells us that the Lord came to Moses to ask him to deliver His chosen people from the slavery of Egypt.

"Now, therefore, go and I will be with your mouth and teach you what you shall speak." (Exodus 4:12)

But Moses resisted and asked the Lord to send someone else who was a better speaker, his brother Aaron. God finally relented and agreed to work with both of them in shared leadership to free His people from slavery.

That didn't happen to Little Black Moses from Lowndes County, Alabama. George was called and George was willing to speak out. The Reverend George Walker Smith was headed for America's promised land – California.

Leaving Pittburgh Seminary, 1956

Golden Hill United Presbyterian Church, 20th and Market Streets

Section Two
Black in a Beach Town

Chapter Four
San Diego Meets George

There was a lazy waterfront, a tiny airport, and a sense of isolation in the San Diego that Irene and I drove through for the first time on June 5, 1956. Here, in contrast to the brick row homes and stately church buildings in Pennsylvania built to shut out snow, were lightweight, wood-frame houses that let in the cool breezes off the bay. Where Pittsburgh was hip and rhythmic, San Diego was sleepy. But I liked it here.

Although San Diego had an overwhelming military presence – in Camp Pendleton, the 26-mile northern buffer against encroaching L.A./Orange County, in North Island and the Naval Amphibious base to the south, Naval Training Center and Marine Corps Recruit Depot just north of downtown and Miramar Naval Air Station to the east – there were relatively few blacks in town. Especially Presbyterian. Especially Republican.

In fact, Irene and I came close to never coming to San Diego. Back in Pittsburgh, the United Presbyterian Church of North America was having a hard time finding a placement for its newly ordained Negro minister. The National Board had a Southern Branch, a Northern Branch and a branch that sponsored the schools. They combed the branches across the United States to find a congregation in need of a black pastor.

There were really only two offers. One was from a church in

Chicago. I did not want to take my young son there. Violence was on the rise, with the Stones and the Disciples receiving a lot of attention. No way was I going there.

The denomination looked hard at the situation in San Diego, where the congregation had requested that the denomination build the Palisades Presbyterian Church in the suburb of Allied Gardens so they could abandon their downtown site at 22nd and Market Streets. White flight. It was happening in communities all across America where downtowns were deteriorating and bedroom communities were becoming the attractive alternative to urban living.

At first, the National Board of Missions of the United Presbyterian Church said that there was no money to both build a new church and buy the old one. But they hadn't counted on the women.

During my tenure in seminary, Irene had worked at the executive offices of the Women's Committee of the United Presbyterian Church of North America. When they heard of our plight, they lobbied the denomination administrator and insisted that they provide the church in San Diego "for George and Irene." The next thing we knew, we had our assignment. The Women's Association provided $50,000 to purchase the church. Our lovely church, with its mission-style spires and arches, became the Golden Hill United Presbyterian Church. Today it is a registered historic landmark

Herb Klein, then-editor of *The San Diego Union*, was a strong Presbyterian, so he made sure that the newspaper announced my coming. There were solid Presbyterian churches in La Jolla, Point Loma and downtown San Diego that understood the importance of their role in the community. The church was much more powerful in civic life at that time than it is today.

My friendship with Herb later developed into a deep one. One of my most vivid memories is the day that Carl Stoke was elected mayor. Herb called me and said, "George, did you hear what happened in Cleveland? Hell! You know, I wanted you elected as the first black mayor of a major city."

"That may be, Herb, but you didn't do anything to encourage it," I told him.

The announcement that San Diego was gaining a black minister to lead a Presbyterian Church in a white neighborhood did not make everybody happy. There was a woman who lived just down the block from the church, Violet Beck, who was greatly offended and started a campaign of letter writing to block us from coming. She had never been to the church, but that did not stop her. Her letters were vicious, sent to the National Board of the United Presbyterian Church. Of course, she probably never knew that we saw a copy of every single one.

It didn't surprise us – or stop us. In the Presbyterian denomination, there is usually a house or "manse" that is used to house the pastor's family. They usually make sure that it is close to the church, probably so they can have your constant attention. We moved into a tidy, two-bedroom craftsman house on a corner two blocks from the church. As we got to know San Diego, we began to appreciate the bright bursts of bougainvillea against the clear blue skies and constant warm temperatures.

The church in the suburbs was not yet ready to occupy. So when we started our services in San Diego, the white pastor and I shared the ministry in the community and took the pulpit on alternate Sundays. I had spoken to dozens of white audiences during my seminary days in Pittsburgh, so it didn't bother me at all to have whites in the service. As I began to do outreach into the community, the pews began to get more colorful. For a full six months, we had a fully integrated church, blacks and whites worshipping, singing and praying together. It was the most integrated church in all of San Diego – there had not been one before and there has not been one since.

Inevitably, the transition period ended. A few Sundays before it came time for the new church to open, one of the Sunday school kids came to see me inside the church after the service.

"Reverend Smith?" she said, "There is a man out there on the patio trying to get people to go to the new church. I heard him…"

She was right. There was a flyer being distributed suggesting church members leave because the whites were moving to eastern San Diego. Phil West, who had been a missionary in Ethiopia for many years, stood outside the front door passing out information about the new church. I was bitterly disappointed.

That was not the only disappointment that met us in Southern California. We had contracted to have certain equipment – chairs, pianos, hymnals and the like – remain at our church after the old congregation moved to the suburbs. This contract was not honored. We were horrified that those wealthy white worshippers took everything they could move to the new church. They didn't see the problem.

That first summer of my ministry, the National Board sent us five college kids, four white and one black, to help with a Vacation Bible School program that would engage the community. They were fantastic. Coming from different parts of the country, they ran the summer program, and built up our Sunday school attendance. They even sang as I tried to get a choir going. I did not allow the detractors to get to me. In fact, I started to laugh at their efforts.

Jesus told a very pointed story to a group of religious leaders who were trying to discredit his message to love your neighbor. "Who is my neighbor?" they asked.

Jesus answered them. A Jewish man was traveling to Jerusalem when thieves overcame him, beat him and left him for dead. At first a priest walked by. He wanted nothing to do with the incident. Didn't want to get involved. He crossed to the other side of the road.

Then one of the injured man's own countrymen came past. He, too, did not want to dirty his hands or delay his journey. That man walked on and ignored the suffering and gasps for help.

Finally, a stranger from Samaria, which was composed of racially mixed families – half Jewish and rejected by the established religion – came by. He immediately went to the aide of the hurt man, bound his wounds, took him to an inn and paid in advance for him to stay as long as he needed.

"Which one," Jesus asked the complacent and arrogant leaders, "was this man's neighbor?"

One by one, Irene and I were beginning to find out who were

our true neighbors.

Slowly I was forming a dedicated group of people to lead my congregation. As a Presbyterian church, we had a very organized worship and followed a number of church traditions and liturgies. Black folk would sometimes come to visit and say, "Why are they down there actin' like them white folk?" I was acting like George Smith. My message was one of dignity, study, faith and activism. My congregation embraced it. Those who didn't were told, "This church supports Reverend Smith. If you don't like it, go someplace else where you can be happy."

Over the years, my church has included some fantastic leaders and the City of San Diego has been blessed by it. My congregation has been willing to get involved. My mandate from God is to preach that Christians are called to serve, not just sit and be comfortable. The average preacher, that old "Christian right" group, never mentions the social gospel. To them, the social gospel is sending some food down to Honduras or someplace. To me that is about as Christian as a skunk I saw run across the street the other day. I'm not the average preacher and I never wanted to be the average preacher.

Faith has to impact a person's political life, economic life, social life and educational life, as well as one's spiritual life. I trained my

70

congregation to receive this gospel and they have stayed with it for over 40 years. Within the first few years of my ministry, I was involved in over 15 boards and agencies, making a difference.

Years after Irene and I first arrived, I saw old Violet Beck sitting at a bus stop as I was walking by. She called out to me, "Reverend Smith! Reverend Smith!" and I walked over to her.

"I just wanted you to know," she said, "that you've done a marvelous job in the community. You've just done a great job."

"Thank you, Miss Beck," I said and walked on.

Big Brother Picnic, 1965

Section Two
Black in a Beach Town

Chapter Five
Conscience of the Community

During our first years in San Diego, jobs for Negroes were available as doormen, bellmen, elevator operators, cooks, housekeepers and caterers. Entrepreneurs had started small businesses along Imperial Avenue, the main street for the black community. We were very interested in bettering our lot. But most homegrown San Diego businesses kept blacks in menial positions. It was terrible.

In those days, most of the decisions about the city's growth, direction, policies and procedures were in the hands of about 150 white men who made up the school boards, commissions, city councils and the board of supervisors. They had come here, started businesses, thrived and, for the most part, tried to make San Diego a better place.

Typical of these was C. Arnholt Smith, an old-style city "boss" who owned one of the local banks and the Padres and wielded enormous power over the outcome of elections and the appointment to boards in the city and county. Other influential city fathers included Andy Borthwick, the head of First National Bank; Elliott Cushman, father of Steve Cushman, the current chairman of the Port District; George Scott, from the Walker Scott department stores; Phil Klaubers, Clinton McKinnon, former Congressman and editor of *The Sentinel*; Bill Quirk, the head of

Pacific Bell, Morley Golden and others.

Once I got the church established, I became more interested in how I could affect community. As I got to know these men who ran the town, they did not shut me out of making contributions. I was one of the most educated Negroes in town, and they did not deny my input. Usually I would go with another black leader to a meeting with one of these whites and bring a request or explain a situation that needed to be addressed. We would say our piece and then one of them would say, "O.K., now get the hell out of here." We had to trust them to enact the changes, and many times they did.

But by the end of the 1950s, these men saw the advantage of having me in a more prominent role in the community. Within a few years, I was on several boards as "the black board member." I didn't care why. It brought me to seats of power that I would never have occupied and expanded my sphere of influence. In the process I earned their respect.

Even so, there were places in San Diego that still openly discriminated against blacks, such as the gracious Lubachs Restaurant and the luxurious Grant Grill, which also banned women from its tables. Several hotels and restaurants did not want blacks as patrons. Dean Bistline, a white educator, would take me with our Hispanic friend, Amando Rodriguez, to some of these "whites only" places that reportedly discriminated. They never once refused to serve me, which would have allowed me to sue them and make quite a bit of money. In fact, I never made one penny for being discriminated against. No matter what I tried.

I think God had another thing in mind.

Many of those with positions of influence believed that black folk, given the opportunity, could be a part of the efforts to make the community a better place. As we entered the decade of the '60s, the need for racial equality was beginning to reach the consciousness of San Diegans. Blacks held sit-ins at Woolworth's organized by Dr. Jack Kimbaugh, who headed the NAACP, but bold placards still stood, forbidding Negroes from being served at their counter. There was nothing to outlaw it. Pockets of discrimination were alive and well. And we knew that most San Diegans felt that we blacks should know our "place."

Our "place" was a very defined residential area when it came to housing. Racial discrimination was not even questioned when it came to housing. Except for a little ghetto in La Jolla inhabited by butlers and maids, black people, by and large, lived south of Market Street. Period. The practice of housing discrimination was called "redlining," which meant that certain areas were black and certain areas were white. Real estate agents were afraid to talk to a black family about the purchase of a property. They would give every excuse possible not to show a house. "There are no Negroes allowed in this area," they would say. There were no fines for discrimination; agents just blatantly practiced it.

In addition, there were restrictive clauses in real estate contracts stipulating that you would not sell to a black person. Housing covenants prohibited blacks and Mexicans from buying in certain areas. In La Jolla, the town council met in a historic meeting until 3 a.m.. to consider letting Jonas Salk, who was Jewish, buy a home in La Jolla. Their "yes" vote crossed a barrier that led to the establishment of the Salk Institute, one of the country's most prestigious scientific institutions. Without the breaking of that barrier, another proud accomplishment of our city – the University of California, San Diego – might never have been established.

Once a black family did move into a neighborhood, agents, even black ones, would walk door-to-door and solicit sales, saying, "Your property values are going to go down, sell now while you can."

By the early 1960s, the federal government had enacted executive orders that reduced discrimination in the defense contracting industry. Middle-class black families came to San Diego to work for the area's great defense corporations – General Dynamics, Teledyne Ryan and others. This diverse and well-paid workforce found that their money was not welcome in some parts of San Diego. I resolved that I would do everything that I could in a peaceful way to help this city get rid of its racial barriers.

The first area to begin to integrate was Valencia Park, a lovely neighborhood with wide, tree-lined streets. Some of my congregation lived there and it was referred to as the "Point Loma of South San Diego." Communities such as Sherman Heights, Golden Hill, North Park and others began to integrate. Successful blacks bought lovely homes that were well landscaped and beautifully appointed. Pride in the community was on the rise. Many of these parishioners were attracted to my ministry because of the dignity of the Presbyterian worship traditions and the intellectual emphasis of my sermons. They became strong supporters of the church.

There was a corner house on a lovely rise of 21st Street in Valencia Park overlooking the city that one of my banker friends told me to take a look at. It had a sweeping lawn and was situated in a beautiful residential neighborhood a little distance from the flat and crowded urban grid where we were raising our children.

The house had been built by a mean and bigoted white man. When he was forced to sell after a divorce, he shouted to the bankers, "I'm never sellin' to any niggers! Never!" Despite that, a black family lived there a few years and took out a $20,000 loan to finish the basement, but lost their means. Then it went to the bank. But bankers only care about one color: green.

"Go see the house, George," said my friend in real estate, Ray Clancy. Of course, we loved it, but they wanted a $2,600 down payment. Where in the hell would I get $2,600?

Harold Logan and I had been appointed to the Mental Health Board. We were on the way to Patton State Hospital in San Bernardino one day. On the long drive, he asked, "How does the Presbyterian Church house its ministers?' His father had been an Episcopalian minister and he told me they had always lived in the worst-looking house in the neighborhood. I told him that the Presbyterian Church encouraged pastors to buy their own homes and build some equity for the family's future. Then I let him know about the house in Valencia Park that was beyond our reach. "Where am I going to get $2,600? I only make $3,600 a year. And besides, a black man getting a dollar loan from these banks would be like tryin' to pull teeth out of a chicken."

"George, why didn't you come to me? Send that real estate

man to my office." The next day he wrote a check for the down payment. Irene and I were thrilled.

We sold the manse on behalf of the Presbyterian Church and helped resolve their financial risk in bringing us to San Diego. Less than a year later I was able to cash in some securities with enough money to repay Harold Logan the down payment. God had it all worked out.

The Fair Housing Act was brought to the California ballot by a black assemblyman, Byron Rumford, as Proposition 14. He brought to the table a new concept: discrimination against Negroes with regard to selling or renting private property should be illegal. The legislation made many of my Republican friends uncomfortable.

Only two Republicans, including George Christopher, mayor of San Francisco, were in favor. Ronald Reagan, who was competing with Christopher for the governorship of California, was against the Fair Housing Act.

A party meeting was called in Santa Monica, with 300 blacks in attendance, to meet with Reagan. The room was filled with prominent African-Americans who were faithful Republicans. We grilled the candidate on his civil rights stance.

The question was asked, "Mr. Reagan, if you had been in

Washington, D.C., how would you have voted on the Civil Rights Act?"

"Why," said Reagan, "I would have voted against it."

He said this three times. I was in the back of the room with Jim Floynoy, a prominent black Republican leader. "Jim," I said, "I've got to say something." So I stood and was recognized.

"Mr. Reagan, you don't know it, but you have really grieved us here today," I said. "We are here to figure out if we should stay in the Republican Party and make a difference. What you have told us here today is that if you had been voting, you would have voted against the second Emancipation Proclamation. I'm glad you weren't here when Lincoln signed the first one, because I would still be in Alabama picking cotton."

His eyes teared with rage. He balled up his fists at George Christopher and stormed off the stage. I found out later that he hissed, "Son of a bitch!" because he felt that Christopher had set him up. All I did was ask an honest question.

Later, back in San Diego, I got a call from San Diego attorney Gordon Luce, a man I greatly respected and who worked on the Reagan campaign.

"George," he said, "I heard about the meeting in Santa Monica. I wonder, the next time Ronnie is in San Diego, would you meet with him?"

I told him I wouldn't mind meeting Reagan. About two weeks later he called and set it up at Kim Fletcher's office in the Home Federal office tower. I decided to bring Dr. John Ford along because I don't like to meet with politicians alone.

"I can make this meeting very short," I said. "Do you really mean to tell us that you would have voted against the Civil Rights Act?"

"George, I'm afraid so," said Reagan. "You can't pass legislation to make me love you."

"Mr. Reagan, that may be true," I answered. "But as Dr. King often said, you can't pass legislation for someone to love you, but you can pass legislation to make it more difficult for someone to lynch you. My friend here, Dr. Ford, is a wealthy man. He tried to buy a lot in Del Mar and was refused. He would have fit just fine in that neighborhood."

"I believe that property rights are sacred," Reagan argued.

"More sacred than human rights?" I was incredulous. "Mr. Reagan, you are going to win this election to be governor, I'm sure. But you are going to win it without my support."

I left. When Reagan did win, the only office I was asked to hold at the state level was with the Mental Health Board, and he ended up closing the mental hospitals and destroying a system that was working to keep disturbed people off the street. Lucky for me, that appointment helped me buy my house in Valencia Park.

Today, blacks with enough money can pretty much buy a house anywhere in San Diego County. As long as they don't bring too many of their friends with them.

It's not too different from my seminary days back in Pittsburgh when my professor warned me about my acceptance by white congregations. A smattering of integration is tolerated. But if the racial balance in a neighborhood tips from minority to equal, let alone majority, I don't think things are much different than they were 50 years ago. A love of equality is not the natural condition of the human heart.

Jesus himself addressed this issue when he said, "How can you say you love God when you hate your brother?" Anyone who says they love God, yet hates their brother, is a liar and a hypocrite!"

For those of you who say you love God, whom you have not seen, how can you say that you hate George Smith, who has never done you any harm? How can you let fear of the color of my skin prevent you from obeying God's call to righteousness?

If you are a person of faith, you have to think about what God would have you do. With God, there is no respecter of persons, according to the apostle Paul. No Greek, no Jew, no male, no female. No black. No white. This was the mission of Jesus Christ himself. He was crucified, buried and rose again. That has been my motivation and, as I have studied the four gospels over and over, I have raised the question, "What did Jesus see as the most important message of his life?" It was to rectify the inability of human beings to love one another.

As sweeping changes ushered in the '60s and '70s, it was no wonder that the social change in racial relations was accompanied by a similar revolution in the Church. The "Jesus Movement" went arm-in-arm with the Civil Rights Movement. Unfortunately, only one of them had staying power.

In response to the many federal laws being passed in the early 1960s eliminating discrimination, I was asked by Joe Sinott of San Diego Gas & Electric to address a convention of about 300 employees from Orange, Riverside, and San Diego counties on the subject of "Equal Employment Opportunity in the Gas Company." It was a fabulous lunch – you know how those top managers can eat. But after the meal I stood up with my five-page, doubled-spaced speech and looked around the room.

"Joe," I said, "you invited me to come here and speak about equal job opportunities in your company. Look at this audience,

Joe. There ain't such a thing in the Gas Company. Here's my speech." I handed it to him. "You can read it Monday when you go to the office.

"See, the only way black George can become an employee of your company is to marry your daughter or your brother's daughter. That is highly improbable. The reason why you don't have equal opportunity in your company is because you leave the hiring of the personnel up to your division heads. All of them are white. There aren't even any Mexicans or women. So a black has as much chance of becoming an employee of your company as a snowball has of existing in hell." Then I sat down.

Joe got up slowly. There was dead silence in the room.

"George has laid something on us today," he said, "and he's right. Now I'm gonna' make some changes. From now on, any SOB that I find discriminating in this company is going to be put out on his ass."

About two months later, I heard footsteps coming toward my office. The man coming up the stairs introduced himself as Joe Foley, and he had just come from Denver to SDG&E. He was hired to reorganize the entire personnel department and make it more equitable.

"I'm telling you," said Foley, "if you find any black folk who want to become employed by the Gas Company, send them directly to me, not to anyone else." Lee Rawlings was the first one I sent and he was hired by Joe Foley of the Human Resources Department. Many more followed. As economic conditions strengthened for blacks, they dispersed into all San Diego neighborhoods, which was the right thing to do.

The old black community from Imperial Avenue has been displaced these days by Mexican immigrants. The neighborhood around my first church at 22nd and Market Streets speaks a different language. Houses have been covered with stucco and painted bright colors, and restaurants serve more tortillas than fried fish. Black families and businesses have moved east to Euclid Street, East San Diego, Lemon Grove and Spring Valley. In a way, it's a shame. Black history is no longer centered in one place, where you could walk around and see where Judge Earl Gilliam lived as a child, or where the clothing stores, markets, eateries and other black-owned businesses thrived.

The "boss" system has also been replaced in San Diego. Outside corporations have come to town, with leadership that isn't dedicated to building up San Diego. Those who would give to the community, in the tradition of the Rockefellers and Carnegies, are no longer doing so. The newer generation has not learned to give, but to "get theirs."

But I didn't see that in 1962. I was struggling for equality like other black men and had chosen my platform for affecting change. It had to happen in the schools.

San Diego School Board, 1963

National School Board, 1977

88

Section Two
Black in a Beach Town

Chapter Six
An Education in Education

By the early 1960s, Irene and I had added two daughters, Joyce and Carolyn, to our family. My activities were invigorating and the church was thriving. We turned our attention to the schools, and what we saw gave us reason to get involved. Although there were hundreds of black children in the San Diego Unified School District, there were few black teachers and no black administrators. American schools were becoming the focus of attention regarding discrimination and prejudice. In 1961, the first black students were admitted to the University of Georgia. In 1962, James Meredith enrolled at the University of Mississippi as armed National Guardsmen looked on.

Many people felt that America's racial strife would only ease through the training and education of a new generation. At the time, I believed it, too.

Basically, all of the members of the San Diego Board of Education in the early 1960s came from Point Loma, Mission Hills and La Jolla. Elections were held city-wide and the voting blocks of those communities ensured that rich whites would become the decision-makers. The tables were stacked against blacks running for office.

So, we decided to turn the tables.

A policy change was set into motion by a committee that

several of us formed, the Citizens Study Committee of the Board of Education, to shift the election of school board members from city-wide to district-wide votes. The school district was divided into five areas: A through E. Candidates would campaign only in their area for the primary, and then the top two candidates would face each other in a run off in the city-wide election. This would ensure that someone who lived in those areas would represent neighborhoods on the Board of Education. A large group of San Diegans, many of them white, supported the change. But many opposed it.

Dr. Frank Lowe, who was serving on the school board at the time, was particularly against the concept. "There are some areas of the city, especially E in Southeast" he said in public, "where I think it may be impossible to find someone qualified to sit on the school board." What an insult.

Ultimately, the measure got the support of the League of Women Voters, the mayor, the city council members and finally San Diegans, who voted it into law. Not long afterward a multi-ethnic group of community members came to meet with me at my home in Valencia Park. Some of them were leaders of the Urban League.

"We want you to run for the District E seat on the school

board," they said. "We can nominate you, and we know that we will outnumber voters in Point Loma, Mission Hills and La Jolla. What do you say, George?"

I had absolutely no desire to run for any office. It was 1963, and there were very few blacks elected to anything. Blacks were suffering beatings and other injustices just to register to vote in my hometown in Alabama. Four little Sunday school girls were killed in a church bombing in Birmingham. The Peace March on Washington, D.C., brought 250,000 people together to hear Martin Luther King Jr. give a speech. "Now is the time to open the doors of opportunity to all of God's children," he said. "We will not be satisfied until justice rolls down like waters and righteousness like a mighty stream."

Perhaps it was time for me to take a risk. I had served on many boards with friends all over the city. San Diego was still riddled with racism, and I knew that there was no other black who would stand a chance. I talked it over with Irene and came back to the group of community members with this message.

"I will not run as a black candidate. If I do that, I am doomed. I will represent the children of this city who are striving for education, may they be in La Jolla or Southeast San Diego. Second, I will not go into debt. That's for sure.

"Finally, I want to organize my campaign with a captain in every community in San Diego."

So we went to work. San Diego was racist to the point that I did not put my picture on any of my campaign literature, nor would I go on television. I included my white friends on my steering committee, which meant I had the most integrated, multi-racial campaign committee in the history of San Diego – even to this day. Most of the downtown leadership, such as Kim Fletcher, of Home Federal; Gordon Luce, of American Savings Bank; Tom Sefton, of San Diego Trust & Savings Bank; and Bea Everson, who saved Balboa Park from ruin, went out to groups around the city to speak on my behalf. Our public relations firm, Wilson and Stodell, had a social conscience and felt the need for diversity on the school board. Hundreds of people worked diligently on my campaign.

I ran on four important issues: funding for the schools, adult education expansion, increased vocational training opportunities, and increasing teachers salaries. The message emphasized the need for quality education for all San Diego children. My own children, Anthony, 11, Carolyn, 6, and Joyce, 4, were my motivation.

My main opponent was David Reed, a 72-year-old, blind white man. That was another great motivator, because defeat would have been so humiliating.

Everyone was on pins and needles at Election Central as the votes came dribbling in – 551,000 votes in all. I beat David Reed by 411 votes.

The Evening Tribune of November 7, 1963, shows a smiling, proud black family enjoying the election results. "He is the first Negro to be elected to the school board, " according to that day's newspaper. Actually, I was the first Negro to be elected to anything in San Diego.

Immediately I went to work with enthusiasm, setting policies and guiding the superintendents into a new era.

After about a year in office, at the end of one of our public meetings, Dr. Frank Lowe went to the podium.

"I have something bothering me," he said. "I want to make a public apology. During the debate over the proposition to hold district elections, I said that there would be an area of San Diego that would not produce a qualified candidate. As far as I am concerned, and I want everyone to know it, there could be no more qualified candidate anywhere on the school board than George Smith."

It wasn't too difficult to right some glaring wrongs. First were the employment practices. The district had fewer than two dozen black teachers and even fewer Hispanic teachers. Yet some schools had 72 percent black and Hispanic enrollment. That had to change.

Where are the ethnic teachers? I asked. Where are the Asians, the blacks, the Hispanics? We can't find them, was the answer. In practice, 75 percent of teacher recruitment was happening at the School of Education at San Diego State College, which rarely admitted blacks.

If you can't find them here, I said, go out and get them.

Even though I was on a very conservative board, I got them to adopt a policy of promoting equal employment. I knew that Ralph Dailard, the superintendent of schools, was very conservative and, in fact, some of the board members had tried to get him fired because they believed in change.

It was an open board meeting when I spoke out. I have never believed in saying anything in private that I could not say in public. There was a sea of white, black and brown faces in the audience. The room was tense.

"This district has been the perpetrator of inequality all these years," I began. "It is time, especially with my represented area educating the overwhelming majority of blacks and Hispanics, to change the tools we are using. We need an inclusive administrative workforce, as well as an all-inclusive teaching force."

The vote was taken and the policy passed. We instructed the superintendent to find programs that would address these needs. After that, every spring the Board of Education sent a recruiter out to the black colleges in the South. I would tell them what colleges to visit. By the time I left the school board 16 years later, there were 700–800 black teachers in the district; I would guess that 90 percent of them came from our recruitment efforts.

There weren't that many roadblocks to diversity, just the fact that any change would challenge the established status quo. One afternoon the vice principals of the district had a meeting at Hoover High School to find out what they could do about "that board member" who was responsible for minority appointments to administrative jobs. Lucky for me that a member of my church, John Curry, left the meeting and came straight to my office.

"You know what they are doing over at Hoover? Trying to see what they can do to stop you from influencing the board!" he said.

They did not see the need for diversity for the sake of the children. It didn't bother me. As long as I had a majority vote and the support of the superintendent, I never let anything else bother me.

Over the next few years I earned the respect of the other board members for my honesty and integrity. One interesting faction – members of the John Birch Society (who were legion in those days in San Diego) – also respected me. A man named Armin Moths was sent from the John Birch Society newspaper, *The Observer*, to monitor the school board meetings. We struck up a marvelous relationship: I wouldn't listen to anything he said.

Armin would often come to my house in the evenings and show me his John Birch literature to convince me of his cause. One time as a board meeting was ending and we were going into executive session, he stepped forward.

"I just want to say something to you. I tell my colleagues that you are the most consistent officeholder I have ever met. Although I think you are always consistently wrong, you are consistent."

A few years later, he got into trouble with a business partner down in the barrio who couldn't pay his taxes. Armin was locked up with the owner, and I got a call.

"George," he said, "can you do me a favor? I need a character letter."

Here's what I wrote:

I have known Armin Moths for many years and I truthfully say that, although I do not concur with his beliefs, he is consistent in his beliefs, he is honest in his beliefs and I honor him for his patriotism.

97

After I got all of my Republican friends to set Affirmative Action goals in hiring, another major issue came to the forefront of the schools. The year that I was elected to the school board, President Kennedy sent federal troops to enforce the right of black students to enroll at the University of Alabama. I knew the unrest that this would cause in the counties of my home state. How would integration affect San Diego?

Racial discrimination had been outlawed by the U.S. Supreme Court in 1954, overturning the "separate but equal" doctrine and acknowledging that "separate educational facilities are inherently unequal." The Supreme Court order had called for school integration "with all deliberate speed." It was the beginning of a social revolution in America. Nonetheless, 10 years had passed in San Diego without much change, so the federal government was stepping in.

Under the sweeping provisions of the Civil Rights Act, signed into law on July 2, 1964, by President Lyndon B. Johnson, schools were ordered to be desegregated. How that was to be accomplished became a topic of active debate for the school board a few years later, just before I became the first black president of the San Diego Board of Education. The wisdom at that time dictated that integration of the schools would only happen when kids from the black schools could be transferred to the white schools.

But first we had to show the need. The Citizens' Committee on Equal Educational Opportunities laid the groundwork in 1965 by conducting a long-term study of the conditions of San Diego schools. When the report was published and presented in August of 1966, it showed a substantial degree of racial imbalance. Just 16 elementary schools served 75 percent of the Negro and Mexican-American school population, it stated. Some of the recommendations included inter-racial camping experiences, building school campuses that would cluster educational facilities and serve a broader neighborhood, redrawing boundaries for a greater ethnic mix, revising standards for textbooks, creating a citizen's "watchdog" committee and, of course, transferring students to other schools.

But don't get that confused with bussing. On August 23, 1966, the school board voted to implement the recommendations of the Citizens' Committee on Equal Educational Opportunities and part of those recommendations specified that parents would provide their own transportation to the transfer schools.

The meeting was packed – and contentious. Stephen Hagan, who had launched a failed election bid for the school board, demanded that the elected representatives listen to the people, not the committee. Jack McPherson presented petitions signed by 533 neighbors fearful that transfers would "destroy the neighborhood school system." But the League of Women Voters of San Diego testified by letter, encouraging the board to take "positive action to reduce racial imbalance in the schools." At the end of the day, the board voted unanimously to allow parents to apply for transfers on the basis of improving racial balance. Two weeks later, 55 such applications had been approved

At the next board meeting, I presented an eloquent and well-thought-out policy statement that called for the "eradication" of racial imbalance. My motion asked the board to concur with the findings of the Citizens' Committee and agree that racial imbalance was "damaging to children and impairs equal educational opportunities in a democratic republic." It asked that the board commit to doing "whatever it can to effect social change" in the community. The policy would have positioned the board to ask other public and private organizations to "join us in creating a community free of prejudice, discrimination, bigotry, racism and segregation." The motion failed for lack of a second.

I was stunned. It was a huge disappointment and disillusionment to see that the board would act to right an educational problem, but would not address the greater social problem. At that time, I kept my remarks brief.

"I'm very disappointed. For the board not to act is most unfortunate. Until the board makes a policy, there is going to be turmoil."

Then I turned to the board members and asked, "Point out to me what is wrong with my statement of policy."

The other board members stumbled out potential problems. Fear of the unknown would raise objections, said Louise Dyer, and it would be best for the actions of the board to convey their stand. Arnold Steele, board president, said that the policy statement "smacks of social change." Frank Lowe said that a policy not drafted by the whole board would be "meaningless."

"Your impatience, George, has led you to great error," said Lowe. "We all know the problem, and are grappling with it. The impression you give is that you are the only one concerned. That is not true."

"George Smith does not do things impatiently," I replied evenly. "You people said three weeks ago we needed a policy statement."

School Superintendent Ralph Dailard intervened. He said that he would be making a public comment on the committee recommendations and that his comment would contain a proposed board policy.

I could not believe that five educators could not endorse the simple policy statement. Here is the whole statement:

We, the members of the Board of Education of the San Diego Unified School District, the duly elected trustees, in order to provide equal educational opportunities for all pupils in this district do hereby confirm that:

We concur with the findings of the Citizens Committee on Equal Educational Opportunities that substantial racial imbalance exists in the district's schools.

We also concur that such racial imbalance is damaging to children and impairs equal educational opportunities in a democratic republic.

Be it therefore declared that it is the policy of this board that racial imbalance be eradicated in this school district.

The board recognizes that there are factors contributing to segregation which may be beyond its immediate control, but we can do whatever we can to effect change.

The board therefore calls upon all other local governmental bodies and private entities whose present policies promote de facto segregation to join us in creating a community free of prejudice, discrimination, bigotry, racism and segregation.

Two days later, on September 9, 1966, my wife became the

first Negro teacher ever to be hired by the school district in National City. It was an empty victory. In Mississippi an incident had occurred where a group of adult men beat a Negro child. It was one of the most degrading stains on our nation. And my board was too timid to call for social change!

The next week I had yet another setback. One of the Citizens' Committee's 39 recommendations was to establish a standing advisory committee on equal educational opportunities that would be proactive in helping the board address problems in the schools relating to racial imbalance. The school board wanted to table this recommendation also. Mrs. Dyer and I abstained from the tabling motion, causing Frank Lowe, Gene French and Arnold Steele to go on record against the advisory committee.

The year before, in 1965, the neighborhood of Watts in Los Angeles had erupted in violence, with days of looting, burning, theft and frustration. The Watts riots were a benchmark of racial unrest in America. Along with Dr. Martin Luther King Jr., who was calling for peaceful resistance, new black voices were emerging. Malcolm X was calling for violence. The Black Panthers were calling for students to protest on campuses across the United States, which, in turn, created unrest among high school students.

When the Watts riots occurred and later, when the Rodney

King riots happened in Los Angeles, San Diego's leaders came to me asking, "How can we keep this from happening here?" and "Let's all bind together." But as soon as the last fire in the last building was out, the white folks forgot all about our coalitions.

So I was quelling riots, yet it was amazing to me that this board didn't even want to hear about racial problems from an advisory committee. Did they want to read about them in the headlines? The police reports? It was frustrating to no end.

The week of October 5, 1966 Superintendent Ralph Dailard reported to the board that an investigation was being conducted by the U.S. Office of Education into charges that our board was violating the Civil Rights Act of 1964. The informal statement of allegations included:

Establishment of attendance area boundaries calculated to perpetuate racial segregation; Selection of new school sites in a manner calculated to perpetuate racial segregation; Discriminatory practices in hiring, placement and promotion of teachers and school administrators; and, failure to maintain equal educational opportunities for schools with high enrollment of minority race children.

"This sort of thing makes my blood boil!" said Arnold Steele. "To think a bureaucrat can come in here and put us on the pan."

"I said the same thing," said Dailard, who reported that officers of the U.S. Office of Education had quizzed him for two hours. "This is the thing that leads to federal control over local school districts."

Dailard said that what really made him angry was that the officials refused to name the person who had made the allegations. Dailard said he handed over 11 documents, including the report of the Citizens' Committee on Equal Educational Opportunities. I wonder if he told them that only 1 out of the 39 recommendations had been approved. As for me, I made a statement to the press: "The district should welcome a federal investigation, since it has nothing to hide."

This situation made me wonder about the power that the U.S. Office of Education could have over a local school board. Maybe it was something worth pursuing.

I started serving on a few California School Board committees to raise my political collateral and also to better serve the children under my jurisdiction in San Diego. My goal has always been to bring good, quality education to kids.

Finally, a legal case made school integration an imperative. Larry Collins, a teacher at Morris High School, brought a lawsuit against the school district. He maintained that the schools south

105

of Highway 8 were predominantly ethnic and, therefore, inferior. He maintained that schools that were "racially isolated" caused the white kids in those schools to have an inferior education.

George Welsch, from Del Mar, was the judge, and it was the greatest debate in the history of the school district. At the end of the day, the court ruled that we make active plans to integrate all schools.

San Diego made creative progress in integrating its schools. We started a program called VEEP, where kids voluntarily took buses to schools of low ethnicity. We also had to address the issue of white parents sending their children to our part of town. We started a MAGNET school at Gompers in mathematics and science. We founded the O'Farrell School of Creative Arts, which brought kids from every area of the city to Southeast San Diego. We had an Olympic magnet for athletic kids.

With all this movement of kids around the city, I was the only school board member with children participating. My kids were intelligent enough to get a good education anywhere. Basically, I contend that there is not a school in the district where, if a kid has a supportive parent and is properly motivated, he or she cannot succeed. When I think back over the dilapidated conditions of the school I attended for the first nine years, I realize that if I could learn then, kids can learn now. But I said to my girls, "Your daddy sat there and voted for it, so I'm going to try and find the best public school out there in Point Loma for you to attend. You go get all the education that they are dolin' out to those white kids and take advantage of it."

Joyce and Carolyn went to Point Loma for elementary and middle school, then Carolyn went to Point Loma High, while Joyce went to Hoover. Only once do I remember Carolyn whuppin' a couple of white boys for calling her a "nigger."

Mary Hubbard, from Miles College in Birmingham, Alabama, gave me this formula: heredity x environment x the times = the development of a person. Irish, Italians and others were all treated as inferior at different places and times. The highly developed person will transcend the formula.

After a number of years, I began to soften my attitude about the workings of school integration – and now I have completely reversed my support. For all the millions of dollars we spent during all those years, I don't think the outcome was commensurate with the input. The transfer kids were never integrated into the life of the schools. Some were even required to stay on the bus until classes started. Once they got to the schools, they pretty much separated ethnically. Society was not, and is still not, that accepting of integration, and I realize that the best way to achieve integration is naturally, through the neighborhoods.

Today the public school has become the whipping boy of the Republicans. I resent that. Schools take too much of the blame for the ills of society. Our schools merely mirror what's happening in society. We live in a violent society. We live in an immoral society. Why are we surprised when these things happen in the schools?

Not that the public school system is perfect. But the parochial system isn't perfect, either. Nor are the private schools like La Jolla Country Day, Bishop's and Francis Parker.

All in all, in the 16 years that I served on the San Diego Unified School District Board of Education, I was president four times. As it turned out, the San Diego board was ahead of the rest of the United States when it came to providing me with opportunity. It took me 11 years of sitting on the National School Board before I got the president's gavel in that organization.

Rev. George Walker Smith & Family,

Joyce, Irene, Anthony, George, Carolyn

Section Two
Black in a Beach Town

Chapter Seven
Election Central

The greatest thing happened to me in 1967, way down here, 13 miles from Mexico. The National School Board reached down and asked if I would join their 20-member board. I was the first San Diegan – and the first black American – to be so honored.

Tom Shannon, the attorney for the San Diego Board of Education, had helped me up this ladder by bringing several statewide board opportunities to my attention. Thurgood Marshall had become the first black Supreme Court justice that year, and two cities, Cleveland, Ohio, and Gary, Indiana, had elected black mayors. I broke the barrier at the National School Board and then worked my way up that ladder as well.

On the national board, I was a director until elected secretary treasurer in 1973, then second vice president in 1974, when I served on several committees of the board. Finally, I was called to be president in 1976.

You would have thought I was being interviewed to join the FBI. But you have to realize the nature of the beast. There are 16,000 school districts and 94,000 school board members in the United States. The National School Board represents them all. Some of them were better than others, but most still had an exclusive mentality. The public schools were educating 97 percent of African-American youngsters, but the board members did not see a reason for inclusionary policies on the board.

The first thing I did as president was convince the rest of the board that the headquarters had to move from Evanston, Illinois, to Washington, D.C. Who goes to Evanston? That's where the Women's Christian Temperance Union was founded, and we had to stay at the Worthington Hotel (where they had met). You can't drink there. That was not a place to conduct politics. If we were going to be in the heart of political life, Washington was where the action was. The board vote was almost unanimous.

During that changeover, we also had to appoint a new executive director. I liked the former one, who had helped me up the ladder, but it was time for change. I thought of my friend Tom Shannon and nominated him for the top post in the organization.

Of course I was not alone. Other board members had nominated colleagues and with a great deal of discussion, we had narrowed it down from more than 200 applicants to 3 people. Tom Shannon was among them. From San Diego he had founded the School Board Attorney's Council, a nationwide professional organization that was very successful. As our final selection meeting wore on, it was nearing midnight and everyone was getting tired and cantankerous. I suggested that we adjourn and choose our candidate in the morning.

The next day, I knew I should not be pushing Tom too hard. Dr. Mack Spears, a black professor from Delloite University in New Orleans, finally said, "Why are we going through this? Each of you knows one of these persons. Why don't we listen to what you have to say about each of them? Then we can take a vote."

First, Jean Tuff from New Hampshire spoke. She had a strong candidate. Then the other board member spoke. Then it was my turn.

"Let me tell you about Tom Shannon," I said, "since I brought his name forward. We have all heard that search firm from Kansas City say they went to San Diego and had gotten some great vibes and some negatives. One of the negatives was that Tom seemed to give the impression that he is a know-it-all. That doesn't bother me. When have you seen a bigheaded Irishman who wasn't arrogant?

"And I have to say this: Tom Shannon is the only person that I have known in my life, in or out of the school district, who could have 12 projects going on at the same time and know the details and status of each and every one anytime you asked him. He knows as much about this organization as anyone here. If he is chosen and you become disenchanted with him, I will sign a disclaimer and you can choose someone among you to come and shoot me."

Tom and I accomplished many good things together as executive director and president of that board. I was able to recruit many more blacks to the committees and to the board. The best part about it was getting to stay at the Georgetown Inn. It was marvelous.

For my inauguration as president, I hosted a reception at the Cow Palace in San Francisco for 4,000 people. I was gloriously happy. Friends from San Diego were there to celebrate with me. Diane Clark Bell and I rocked the dance floor.

When my term was over, I flew down to Houston, Texas, to hand over the gavel. There they gave me an award and said, "You have saved this organization, George. Thank you." I was still happy.

What my presidency proved to an American institution was that leadership comes in all colors. With 99 percent of the 94,000 school board members being white, they were amazed that George Walker Smith could exert leadership over the organization.

People can't ignore intelligence too long. I am not a confrontational person, but I earn respect. When you have an attitude of service, your leadership cannot go unnoticed. The Bible says that he who would be great should be the servant of all. If you realize that you are there to serve the Lord and not lord your position over people, you'll right some wrongs. And your door will always be open and your phone will always ring. Don't seek peoples' votes if you don't want to serve them. This attitude caused me to be known as the most revered school board member this city has ever had.

So, you see, I haven't just been little black George raising hell in San Diego. I've raised hell all over.

The public school system is the last real democratic institution in the country. The school systems of this nation must be democratic. Private schools can pick and choose who gets enrolled, but in public schools, students are enrolled based on where they are and what their needs are. Jerry Saunders, head of the United Way, told me that people who used to give to social service agencies are now giving to causes that are already rich. This is a dangerous trend. Bill Gates and Hewlett Packard have offered money to the San Diego Unified School District on the condition that Alan Bersin's contract be renewed. Although I admire what Gates is doing in Africa and with regard to the AIDS epidemic, I do not think he should be involved in local politics. I think it is unethical for the district to accept this money.

When I was first on the San Diego Board of Education, almost 35 years ago, there was a bitter debate over the acceptance of federal money. Many fought against it, citing discomfort with the fact that outsiders could dictate policy to the local schools. I supported it because those policies were centered on inclusion and outlawing discrimination. When we voted to accept federal money, it came rolling into our schools and accomplished things that the San Diego tax dollar alone could never have accomplished.

Is it the same? Not at all. Private dollars and wealthy, privileged donors should not dictate policies of the public schools. Let them donate to private institutions.

For 18 years I headed the United Negro College Fund and raised over $31 million for that agency. Less than a dozen contributors came from San Diego. That is pathetic. We are lagging behind. More than 500 San Diego students are attending those Southern schools and most of them don't come back because the job opportunities are elsewhere. That is where private donations are welcomed.

Elected board members and appointed superintendents should only be beholden to their tax-paying constituents. Otherwise, there is no system of checks and balances. I have no doubt that such privatization will lead to an inferior education for poor children. It opens the door to private clusters dictating the ideologies of the public schools. That's a door that should be held firmly shut.

***

By 1970, the political scene in San Diego had opened up a bit. The scars of President Kennedy's assassination, Robert Kennedy's assassination, Medger Evers and Martin Luther King Jr.'s martyrdoms were beginning to heal. Watergate had yet to rear its ugly head, and hope was beginning to spring up in hearts here and there.

San Diego had not yet undergone its own version of a power cleanup. I had served on the National School Board and many statewide commissions, as well as dozens of local boards. For three years I had served successfully on the school board and was slated to be president. Early in 1970, I had been appointed to serve with the White House Conference on Children and Youth.

My philosophy was that every level of government needed to have representation from all ethnic groups. I had proven that I was electable and looked at the possibilities of further challenges. I began listening to Jack Walsh and Harry Shidell – a progressive block on the San Diego County Board of Supervisors. An open seat was coming up and I decided to throw my hat into the ring. There were about six other candidates and I ended up facing attorney Jim Bear in the runoff after the primary, when the field was narrowed down to the two of us.

I had a great team. One of the men I admired most was Jim

Copley, owner of the *San Diego Union* and *Evening Tribune* papers. He gave me $500, good money in those days. It was the first time that he had ever donated to a political campaign. I was assisted by Frank Thornton, Dick Silberman and Bob Petersen, all of whom believed in diversity and supported my campaign.

C. Arnholt Smith was another matter. My fellow Republican looked me in the eye and said, "George, you know we all love you. But there are some people around town that feel you will be siding with Jack Walsh and Harry Shidel on lots of issues."

"If you don't know by now that George Walker Smith is his own man," I said, "then I don't want your money."

"Oh, now, now," he said. "We're going to support you."

He gave me a check for $500. He gave Jim Bear a check for $1,500.

Later, Dick Silberman said, "You know what he's afraid of? Jack and Harry have been working against C. Arnholt Smith controlling all of the government commissions. He knows that when it comes down to it, you won't be controlled by him, but will look at the qualifications. You will change all of that."

Years later, Smith was brought to his knees by a young, hotshot district attorney named Ed Miller. Miller ended up bringing his own form of control to San Diego until the current district attorney,

Paul Pfingst, defeated him after more than 30 years in office.

In the South Bay I had the support of all the major civic leaders – Kiwanis, Rotary, etc. – except for two: Cal Morgan, the mayor of National City, and George Waters, the councilmember. Llowell Blankfort, publisher of the *Chula Vista Star-News*, was the captain of my campaign there. He went to talk to these key people on my behalf.

With Mayor Cal Morgan, Llowell said, "All of us know Jim Bear and I don't see how in the world you can support him. Can I get your endorsement of George?"

"I'm from Missouri," said the mayor, "and I just can't bring myself to support a Negro."

George Waters had the same racist response. "Oh, no!" he told Llowell. "I can't vote for that pork chop!"

Not all of the leadership of San Diego was that bad.

Pete Wilson, who was an Assemblyman for the 76th District at the time, took me around to areas where I had lost in the primary, such as Serra Mesa, Linda Vista, National City and Chula Vista. We walked those areas with a photographer from *The Sentinel*. On the Sunday before the election, there was a large story in the paper.

On Monday, however, the day before the election, six black

Democrats, financed by Jim Bear, sent a letter to every registered Democrat in the district. "Don't vote for George Smith," it said. "He's a Republican."

Tuesday night, Election Central was again a heated and raucous playground for political hopefuls. Parades, banners, signs and handwritten election results were posted every few minutes. At the end of it all, I had lost by less than 1,000 votes.

"George, you are not going to run for another office," said my wife. "If they don't see the value of having a black supervisor now, then they never will."

Since then I have not run again for office, but have been in the sweet position of supporting or withholding support from others. It feels much better.

When you run for political office, you find out who your true friends are. You find out who is genuine and who is not. Some people can really hurt you when you put yourself out there for votes. But you can't let that get you down. You have to get over the hurt and not take it personally. The greater victory is not in being fallen, but in getting up and going on.

Many years after this election, I was speaking at a prayer breakfast in National City, and when I got up to speak, I noticed that George Waters, who was now mayor, was sitting in front of me.

"George," I said, "I was thinking of moving to National City so I could run against you for mayor. You told my campaign manager once that there was no way you could bring yourself to support 'that pork chop.'"

"I give you credit for one thing: At least you associated me with the best part of the pig."

The audience was stunned.

Being in the public eye also makes you aware that so much of the betrayal by others is simply based on the color of your skin. The main reason that I lost, in spite of the support of Pete Wilson and Llowell Blankfort and Jim Copley and other white leaders, is that I am black. That's it. I don't care how poor or how ignorant the average white man is, he still thinks that he is superior to a black man.

If I'd had my 'druthers, I'd have been white and rich.

If you follow San Diego, you probably already know how I feel about most matters, because I have made that clear in a weekly gathering for over 30 years. If you don't believe it, let me invite you down for a little talk and some catfish, baby.

The Catfish Club brought political discussion into the community.

122

Section Two
Black in a Beach Town

Chapter Eight
Welcome to the Catfish Club

In the Gospel of John, the disciple tells the story of Jesus' life, death and resurrection from the perspective of a close friend. After Jesus' death and resurrection, he appeared to his followers who waited in fear in the upper room. Eight days later, he appeared to them again because of Thomas, who had doubted, and said to him, "Take your finger and trace the scars of my hands, where the nails were driven. Take your hand and place it into the wound in my side, where a sword was thrust into me." Then Jesus said, "Blessed are they who did not see me, and yet believed."

Then again, a third time, Jesus manifested himself to the disciples. They had been out all night fishing. Hadn't caught one fish. As dawn broke, they heard a man call out, "Cast your net on the other side of the boat!" They tried it and caught 153 fish in their small net. As they dragged it to shore, Jesus had the coals laid out and already burning, warming up the bread. Then he cooked them up some fish, and served those cold, hungry, discouraged men. And it wasn't until they had experienced his power, and their stomachs were full and satisfied, that he challenged them: "Follow me."

When I first established the ministry at 22nd and Market at Golden Hill United Presbyterian Church, I had two friends from the membership. One was a postman, Oscar Pendleton, and the other, Ben Holman, was a fireman. On their days off, they would come around to the church and take up my time.

Once a year, Ben would go up to Utah with some of his fireman friends to fish. One day, Oscar and I said, "You know, Ben is always telling us about all these fish, but he never brings back any fish. We're going to tell his wife that something is goin' on. He says he's fishin', but where's the fish?"

The next time we got together I had a surprise for them. I went into the church kitchen and cooked up some catfish, the old Alabama way, with cornmeal. It became a tradition. One day a week I would go to People's Fish Market and look for fish to fry. We would meet, eat and tell lies. After a few months, we decided to call ourselves the CF Club, for Colored Folks Club.

I had been to the Rotary, the Kiwanis and the other clubs in town. In fact, I was the first black to be in the Kiwanis in the entire United States. I had some white friends who submitted my name to join the Southeast San Diego group. The local members said, "No, we can't have any black in our club!"

So, the president wrote letters to every headquarters in America, asking for a policy regarding Negroes. They all said, "No." At the San Diego club, half the members threatened to quit if I joined and half the members threatened to quit if I was not admitted. They voted me in and only three members left the club. I spoke out at the first meeting I attended.

"I understand that you lost a few members," I said. "And those were members that I wouldn't want to be with anyway."

They are probably dead now. And gone to heaven.

At the Colored Folks Club we did not have any such foolishness. Every Friday, I would cook up catfish, fried with cornmeal, and add baked beans and potato salad. Irene would make dessert.

After a while, folks like police chief Bill Kolender, Pete Wilson, Dr. Tom Goodman, who was the superintendent of schools, and Judge Earl Gilliam began to drop by. They came to listen and to learn about the concerns of our community. Then I said, "Look at this group. There should be more to it. Let's make it into a public forum whereby people of every stripe can hear more about the issues, and hear from politicians who want us to vote for them."

The Club started to grow and get a reputation.

This threw us into a dilemma.

"We can't call it the Colored Folks Club with all these white boys coming," someone said.

"If we don't let women come," said Judge Gilliam, "I can get into trouble for discrimination."

Artie Shaw, a news reporter who was part of the group, came up with the solution.

"We've already got the 'CF' established. Let's call it the Catfish Club."

It was a good solution. That was 32 years ago.

Now the Club is integrated and most politicians ask me if they can come and speak to the 150–300 members who care about the community. We've seen them all – Lundgren, Feinstein, Boxer, Gray Davis and local leaders like Malin Burham.

But I'll tell you what bothers me. Politicians come to the Club because they know that I have friends all over the city. As soon as they get elected, they don't come anymore. I invite them to share their opinions, no matter what stand they take. When they are elected, they forget that they came seeking our support.

I have a problem with that. This is one city. Each representative should represent the entire city, not his or her own little district. That's the way I served at the school board, caring about all the children throughout San Diego, not just in District E, and that is how they should serve. We are not a splintered city, and the concerns of the Catfish Club should be the concerns of the entire community. Speakers think that they have to come to the Catfish Club with a speech addressing black folk. They should come with a message for all the citizens of San Diego – white, black, red, yellow or brown.

Of course the speakers also have to be prepared to be put on the spot, and some refuse to come. During the district attorney's race in 2001, Mike Aguirre and Bob Ottalie came, but Paul Pfingst refused. I've wanted to roast Bruce Henderson, but he has turned down my invitations. That may, in fact, be a good decision if you can't support your point of view.

For instance, Dan Lungren came to the Catfish Club and it was very obvious that he should not be running for governor of a diverse state. He talked a lot about Notre Dame and his Catholic upbringing, for some reason. Then he said, "Everyone should be pulling themselves up by their bootstraps."

I rose and looked at him squarely. "What about those of us who don't have boots?"

Michael Huffington came to the Club during his first run for office, which was for a seat in the U.S. Senate representing California. His philosophy and thoughts were so far out that it appeared he knew absolutely nothing about politics, issues or running for office. He said he would do away with the welfare system and have the churches and social agencies take care of everyone.

"Sir," I said, "you are a privileged character. Have you never thought about what the constitution means when it says government of the people, by the people and for the people?"

Afterward I made him an offer. "If you want to come down here, I will take my personal time to sit with you so you won't sound so completely stupid as a senatorial candidate."

He was grateful and thanked me.

Recently I have become very disillusioned with representatives from city and county government. When local politicians come to the Club, I ask them two questions. First, I say, "Are you going to make sure that you make yourself available to the total city? Will we see you again here?" They always say, "Yes." And then we never see them again.

Secondly, I ask, "Will you get some diversity on your staff?"

They don't. Most blacks supported Ron Roberts in the last mayor's race, but he doesn't reflect that in his staff. Mayor Murphy has a few. Aside from George Stevens in the 4th District, there are very few blacks staffing the San Diego City Council. Those opportunities need to be extended to a community that agrees to support a candidate.

I'm the same person after an election that I am before an election. I think that the Club can help politicians keep in touch with the pulse of the community. Isn't that what they want?

For instance, Pete Wilson, whom I once considered a friend, lost touch with the community. He pandered his integrity in an attempt to win the nomination for the presidency by supporting Proposition 209, which rolled back Affirmative Action. This was not the Pete Wilson I had known and supported.

Pete and I had been close friends for many years. He helped me in my race for the San Diego County Board of Supervisors, and I gave the invocation at both of his gubernatorial inaugurations. Pete played upon an element in our country that does not believe in fairness and justice. They don't want to see me, a black man, get nothin'.

I never met a white man yet who lost his job to a black man because of affirmative rights. I got one of the most effective Affirmative Action programs passed on the school board and it passed because it is a good program. It says to the public, "Yes, we have sinned in the past, but we're going to open up the doors. If you're not qualified, you don't get in, but we're gonna at least open that door." You see what I'm saying? It gives hope. Hope is the greatest thing that a person can have. One you lose your hope, you're done for.

Wilson, however, turned his back on all that I had worked for. He had the support of Ward Connelly and Connelly was later rewarded with a seat of the Board of Regents of the University of California. Wilson should be ashamed. Connelly benefited from preferential treatment his whole life. Now that he has made his million dollars and has a white wife, he wants to eliminate the opportunity for others?

Connelly is also supporting the Racial Privacy Act, which is circulating to get on our ballot in 2004. He says it will create a color-blind society. That's ridiculous. How are you going to create that through laws? How does racial privacy relate to a black person? It's pretty hard to keep my race private, isn't it? This is a racially divisive issue.

I support the ballpark for the Padres, and most of the black community has supported John Moores. He has been a very, very fair person. But John Moores should have paid more attention before he offered his home for a fund-raiser for the Racial Privacy Act. He sits on the Board of Regents with Ward Connelly and he has let that take the place of an honest discussion with the black community. He could have had that discussion at the Catfish Club.

Of course, there are some who use the Catfish Club for their own ends. Congressman Bob Filner got his start in politics by attacking a very dear friend of mine, Dorthea Edmondston, whom he defeated for a seat on the school board. That was his springboard to a city council seat, and then Congress. Filner once would do anything to get elected. He's visited the Catfish Club many times.

Now he has learned not to be a manipulator, he has said. I hope that it was not rhetoric, but what else do you have to work with? There is no Republican who will mount a significant challenge for his seat.

George Mitrovitch, who operates the City Club, supports the Catfish Club and has even given me some awards. But I sometimes think he comes to our club to get ideas for his own. For some, it has become a racial palliative.

The Catfish Club has unquestionably had a positive impact on San Diego, however. It's the only place of its kind where people of all backgrounds can come and feel comfortable. It's on the cutting edge of discussion about what is good and what is bad in the community.

I don't fry the catfish anymore. And, through the generosity of Channel 10, KNSD, we meet at their studios off 47th Street every Friday at noon instead of the basement of the church. It's still active, still relevant and still the most important forum for finding out the truth about issues affecting all of San Diego. It has expanded its outreach to a multi-ethnic constituency.

Come. Be fed. Be satisfied. And then be challenged.

George presenting the graduation address to a class of firefighters.

Section Three
Let My People Go

Chapter Nine
Law & Order

In the early days of my life in San Diego, the police department was a very racist organization. Standing like a mission near the waterfront, its tower and arches looking stately and dignified, the police headquarters was actually the façade of a completely racist enterprise. All the officers were white.

There was a lumberyard just south of Market Street. It used to be standard operating procedure that when a white police officer arrested a black man, the officer would go behind the lumberyard and beat the devil out of him before taking him down to the station. Police brutality was the norm.

Ben Cloud was the first black police officer in the region. He was hired in El Cajon and bought several properties there. His son was one of the first black Navy commanders, and he is an outstanding member of that community.

Once black officers were hired in San Diego, they were expected to keep the peace in the Negro community. They were not allowed to arrest a white person, and were only assigned to Imperial Avenue. It was very humiliating.

Tall, light-skinned Jasper Davies was one of those officers, and he suffered the ridicule of the rest of the force. When things got out of hand, there was no backup for him. When things were quiet, he was accused of hiding crimes from the others. Chief

Jansen would walk up and down and say, "Jasper, what's going on down there! Things are pretty calm. You, nigger, you know there is stuff going on down here that you won't tell me."

Officers Cooney White and Johnny Williams were members of my church, and I would sit and listen to their stories. When they were done, they had tears in their eyes. The situation was intolerable.

Justice can be arbitrary and I have experienced both sides of the equation. Once, during our early years in San Diego, my wife and I were driving home at night after visiting with some friends in Point Loma. We were coming down Harbor Boulevard. A policeman saw that I was black and pulled us over.

"Why did you stop me?" I asked. "I don't drive fast, I drive slow."

"What were you doing in Point Loma?" he asked.

"It's none of your business," I said. "If I did something wrong, take me to jail."

The next day I reported the incident to the chief of police. I have not had that experience again.

On the other hand, years later, I was returning from a meeting in La Jolla and this time, I was speeding. Again I was stopped. When the officer saw that it was Rev. George Walker Smith, he waved me on. But if I had been driving home after catering one of those La Jolla parties or cleaning one of those La Jolla hotels, I would have had the book thrown at me.

Racial profiling has been going on since I have been in the world. It's wrong. Black folks are considered crime-committers and law-breakers. That is one of the saddest things in this community.

Good-hearted whites, as well as blacks, fought police brutality, beginning in the early 1960s. Our city was too beautiful to let injustice reign and we all knew it, even then. City Manager John Lockwood recruited me to be the first chairman of the Citizen Advisory Review Board, which provided oversight of police procedures. I never sought subpoena power. People, especially police officers, do not want to be made to do something. The advisory board worked commendably. It continued to be supported by City Manager Jack McGrory as well and it continues to this day. Police know that there are citizens looking over their shoulders in case of rank injustice. For a city of its size, San Diego probably has one of the cleanest police departments in the nation.

During days of the civil rights unrest and the rioting in other cities, San Diego leaders have sought me out to try to keep the black community from rioting here. The day after South Central burned, George Mitrovich came to my office and we formed the Coalition for Racial Equality. A delegation of Clint McKinnon, Bill Quirk and I were sent to other cities across the United States to see what solutions were working. We reported back to the powers that be and they immediately put up money to create programs that would address the social ills.

After the Watts Riots we formed the Urban Coalition.

It kept the peace.

San Diego has never had riots comparable to other cities of our size. We have worked hard to make sure that those things won't happen here.

Not that it is perfect.

San Diego had a close call with rioting during the trial of Sagon Penn, a young black man who shot a police officer and a ride-along citizen when he was threatened with arrest and treated brutally by police. Here was a young black man who was experiencing complete hatred of police officers. I, myself, could not sit on a jury to find him guilty or not guilty. He came to my church looking for counsel and guidance, but was so psychologically afflicted that it was difficult to help him. He recently died, still damaged by the incident.

In 1992, the acquittal of the white officers who had beaten

Rodney King left San Diegans simmering, but we did not burn our communities as they did in Los Angeles. Within five years, the Los Angeles Police Department had to undergo a complete cleanup, revealing evidence of rampant racism, evidence-planting, lying on the witness stand and corruption at every turn. The police force in San Diego had long ago cleaned up its act.

The entire black community has been angered by other recent incidents of racial hatred, such as the beating of a young black man by whites in Santee, the police shooting of a black man in Pacific Beach and the murder of black boys standing on the street by other boys. Children killing children over race.

When you have folks coming together with different backgrounds, you will always have prejudice. What you have to do is create an atmosphere where it is unacceptable to act on those prejudices. That is how to keep the peace and beat back injustice. I sat on the search committees that brought Police Chief David Bejarano, a Hispanic, and former Fire Chief Robert Osby, a black, to the top posts of their departments. These exemplary leaders have gone a long way to dispel prejudices.

There have been a number of blacks who didn't buy my basic philosophy of being a mediator, rather than always raising Cain. Yet some of these same people now thank me. I want to thank you for what you've done in changing attitudes and reaching out to people, they say. Getting with those who were in a position to do something for us, gaining their respect, and showing them the best our community has to offer has been valuable, they say. That has been my motivation. To dispel the erroneous opinions of white people and break down the prejudices. I have devoted my life to that.

Most whites think that any black who speaks confidently and forthrightly is arrogant. They want you to come to them bowing your head and scratching your rear end. I have never done that – and never will.

When Pete Wilson was governor of California, he appointed my friend Gladys Calvin to a board. She was catching the 7 a.m. plane to Sacramento from San Diego one morning when six guys behind her started talking about me.

"That George sure can be arrogant," one said.

Another said, "That may be true, but that is a man you have got to respect."

Gladys turned around and hollered, "You got that right!"

George Smith doesn't ask anybody to love him, but you've got to respect him.

Today the San Diego police department is integrated; the

Citizens Advisory Review Board on Police Practices is still operating and still reviewing cases. I don't think they have as much clout as they used to, but the mechanism is in place. Racial profiling has been studied and data is being gathered to see if it can be proven.

But any young black person knows that it takes place every day. Any black maid who is suspected of stealing, any black mother riding the trolley who is charged with not having a ticket, any black worker who carries out his duties while his white colleagues sit and chat, any black student who doesn't get called on, or any black executive who gets accused of preferential treatment because of race – these people know the truth.

Racial discrimination is a condition of the human heart. I've given up on people having a change of heart. It grieves me greatly to say that. The only thing that can change the human heart is God Almighty. Unfortunately, His church has failed Him.

The congregation moved to Christ United Presbyterian Church, 3025 Fir Street.

Section Three
Let My People Go

Chapter Ten
The Church's Evil Secret

If there is any encouragement in Christ, if there is any consolation of love, if there is any fellowship of the Spirit, if any affection and compassion, make my joy complete by being of the same mind, maintaining the same love, united in spirit, intent on one purpose. Do nothing from selfishness or empty conceit, but with humility of mind, let each of you regard one another as more important than himself; do not merely look out for your own personal interests, but also for the interests of others.

Paul's letter to the Philippians Chapter 2, 1–4

The only reason I am sittin' here today is because of my spiritual faith. It is rooted and grounded in what I understand was the mission and goal of Christ himself. He was killed by crucifixion, buried and rose again. That has been my motivator and my philosophy. I don't have anything else to hang my hat on.

Having studied over and over again the four gospels, which describe the life of Jesus, I see that our Lord addressed the climate of his day politically, economically, socially, educationally and, above all, spiritually. I have shaped my ministry to involve myself in those same areas of life. My greatest disappointment has been in the spiritual communities of San Diego, both black and white. They are good at perpetuating organized religion and completely failing to change hearts. Religion has had a lot to do with racism

144

and separatism, which is innate and ingrained in humanity.

Politically, the church is completely missing the point. Economically, the church should be out front, pushing economic opportunity for everyone, but it sits back and does nothing. Socially, the church is still the most segregated institution that we have in our society. Educationally, the church has lost ground in supporting quality education for all children. Spiritually, people have become lost.

I don't know what will solve this problem. I don't know what will breach the schism between the church and the human heart, but I do know that is the command of Christ – to breach the schism.

I take my marching orders from Jesus Christ. Jesus is concerned about people. Period. And it doesn't matter what their status may be.

But instead, I see the church becoming very irrelevant in the lives of the people in this nation. The church is too busy perpetuating itself. The Lord said, "He who would save his life should lose it, for my sake." The church is not willing to lose anything, to risk anything.

I have never been a person who was happy with playin' it safe. Someone has to say and do certain things for society to progress. Whether it is politically, economically, socially or educationally, someone has the opportunity to be the beacon for the whole world. I have seized that opportunity whenever I could and have trained my parishioners to go forward and make a difference.

I know that it can be done because I've experienced it within the last year.

As evil and as devastating as September 11, 2001, was, something good came out of it. More than ever before in the history of this nation, the American people – all of us – were on the same page. Whether democrat or republican, we were together; whether rich or poor, we united to give. Socially, we forgot what color we were.

Religiously, we were flocking to the churches. Everyone was praying. "God Bless America" was sung by people who had never before uttered His name.

Despite this, I sense one of the seven deadly sins in America – selfishness. All in all, our concern was about the 280 million people in our own country.

Andy Rooney is what I consider a solid-thinking individual. About a month after the crisis of 9/11, he said, "You know, I'm havin' a little problem. I want God to bless America, but it has become a fad."

146

As a Christian, you know it has. Why have we not thought to say, God bless other nations, too? Are we so selfish that we only want God to bless America? Why would we want a God who would only bless us?

A little over six months have passed since the attacks. Church attendance is back to normal. We in this country use God as a safeguard, as an electric appliance: we plug Him in when we think we need Him. As soon as we don't need Him, we unplug Him. God will not tolerate that.

I guess I'm like the old Baptist preacher down south. For seven straight weeks, he preached the same sermon. The church members went to the deacon and the deacon went to him and said, "Reverend, you got to preach something different."

He said, "You go back and ask them if they have stopped sinning those same sins. If they have, I'll stop preaching the same sermon."

My theology teaches me about a caring God. In the Old Testament, it shows clearly how He dealt with His "chosen folks." When they obeyed Him, they were prosperous. When they deviated from the law that He laid down, He dealt with them, naturally or militarily. He cared for them and disciplined them like a mother and father. He hasn't changed His character.

147

It has been difficult for me to remain a Christian when I see the hypocrisy around me. I'm a black Christian because I do cherish my faith and hope – the faith and hope that I have found in Jesus Christ. If I had to base my faith and hope on blacks or whites, I would say, "The Hell with it!" like most of our kids are saying today.

Christ said, "There is neither Greek nor Jew, male or female."

Paul, in the letter to Philemon, said, "The slave Onesimus has made a commitment to follow Christ, treat him as a brother, no longer as slave and master."

Christ changes the equation.

Racism is based on fear. To get at that, we have to first understand the nature of our fear. What are we afraid of? That which we don't know. It's like approaching a baby. If he doesn't know your face, he will cry and scream. If he knows you, he will let you hold him to your breast and he will play with your nose.

Perfect love, says the scripture, casts out fear.

Over the 45 years that I pastored the Golden Hill and the Christ United Presbyterian Churches, I have had a cadre of solid supporters who believed in my interpretation of what the gospel is all about.

I want to thank my congregations for standing by my ministry and me. No pastor has been more blessed.

Since my retirement from the ministry, I have been visiting other churches. Most of the time, my wife and I are the only blacks worshipping. That is against the gospel of Christ. Many times, we walk into a church and the people ignore us and do not say "Hello" or "Welcome." Later, from the pulpit, the pastor will acknowledge me, then everyone claps. This is simply hypocritical.

The Bible says that the time is drawing near when we will all be divided. Jesus Christ will separate the sheep from the goats. We won't be judged by our color, but by the love of Christ that we have in our hearts; the love that we have shared with others. And to the many religious leaders who will be rattling the gates of Heaven to get in, as Jesus says in his parable, God will have a simple reply: "I know you not."

What will God say to you, baby?

Irene Smith, 2002

Section Four
A Word in Edgewise

Chapter Eleven
Preacher's Kids

I am the oldest of the Preacher's Kids. First of all, I would like to thank God for the blessings that He has given me throughout my lifetime as the PK of Rev. George Walker Smith. It's an honor to share some positive experiences with respect to his life and times.

Growing up with my father was special, not only having a minister as a father, but also having a politician as a father. The countless number of prominent individuals I've met in my lifetime has been a treat in itself. Watching the daily news and seeing your own father on television was very special.

Some of our greatest times together happened while I was in elementary school. Every Sunday during football season when the team was playing in San Diego, my father and I would change clothes in his church office and go down to the Charger games at Balboa Stadium.

Those were great times.

And yes, church was a very big part of our lives on a weekly basis: youth choir, youth group, user board, communion server, feeding the homeless and anything else that the "first family" needed to do to support the congregation. To have been born a Preacher's Kid is truly the best blessing a kid could have received.

How many kids do you know who have their father's signature

on both their diploma *and* their marriage license?

Anthony T. Smith

***

We were asked the following question:

What is it like to be raised as children of a prominent African-American minister who happens to be the first African-American elected to public office in the City of San Diego and who has made it his life's work to remedy the injustices suffered by all people, particularly people of color?

Our response is as involved as the question, and you certainly cannot consider any particular aspect of our father's life without considering the entire package. We have been raised with a strong faith in God. We were fortunate to have been part of the development of a church from its infancy. Golden Hill Presbyterian Church was established during a time that the demographics of the city were changing – blacks were moving in and whites subsequently began to move out.

This is significant because the community outreach for the church resulted in our interacting with many young African-American families of the same approximate age and income. Those

153

families became the foundation of our social life in our early years and have become lifelong friends.

Among our church friends, we weren't treated any differently as PKs – we were all just friends. I know that this was at the insistence of our parents. We never had an attitude of superiority. Looking back, our father's respect for the egalitarian aspect of the ministry was instilled in his children. It was a valuable lesson, one that we carry with us to this day.

As our father began being referred to as a "civic leader," and gained a broader field of influence, we began to feel what it was like to grow up with someone of prominence. This increased after he was elected to the Board of the San Diego Unified School District. By that time, we had moved from Sherman Heights to Valencia Park, a middle-class African-American neighborhood.

In school, it didn't take long for the staff and administration to find out who our father was. The reception we received from them was mixed; it ranged from wonderful and encouraging to purposeful antagonism, which we now know was indirectly aimed at our father. But we didn't know that when we were children.

Family structure was very important to us. Growing up, we were required to eat dinner together, to be inside by the time the streetlights were on and to do well in school. That we were going to college was never debated. Our parents led by example – both were college graduates, and the three of us followed their lead and received college degrees.

As children of a Presbyterian minister, we were encouraged to be very open in our thoughts and in dealing with people from all walks of life. Again he led by example. Our father's friends ranged from sanitation workers to many prominent local, state and national leaders. He discoursed with presidents and his children with the same passion.

We have many loving memories of our childhood, from active participation in the church to our father's political campaigns, from the school busing programs to the time mother was attending a retreat and our father attempted to comb our hair. We would like to take this opportunity to say, "Daddy, stick with your day job!"

But if our hair didn't turn out too good that day, many other things in our lives turned out great, thanks to our mom and dad.

Joyce L Yeldell

Carolyn Y. Smith

Neil W. Brown, George Wlaker Smith, President Russell Spry Williams
Mary Holmes College, West Point, Mississippi, Doctor of Divinity, 1997

Section Four
A Word in Edgewise

Chapter Twelve
Don't Quote Me

Over the years, I've been quoted in numerous articles about all kinds of issues. Here are some of the best quotes from *The San Diego Union* and the *Evening Tribune*, as well as the merged publication, *The San Diego Union-Tribune*. Feel free to share these with others.

November 29, 1967

San Diego has forestalled race riots by improving its community relations. The greatest advantage of programs, especially employment programs, is to instill pride. Too often a poverty program makes people proud of being poor.

August 9, 1969

The Negro clergyman does, however, tend to side with those who say that if this country could put a man on the moon it can do more to eliminate social and economic injustice at home.

I rejoiced with all other Americans when our men landed on the moon. I was proud that once we could make up our minds to do something, we could do it. But there are many baffling problems here (poverty, education, housing, race) on earth, however, to which we should make an equal commitment. Sure it's more difficult to create peace and justice on earth, but to make any progress at all requires a vast national commitment that I, for one, haven't seen yet.

June 18, 1970

During the 16 years the Rev. George Walker Smith has been on the San Diego Board of Education, he has been called many things. Tight-lipped, however, is not one of them.

It doesn't bother me what people think. A lot of people stand on the outside, criticize the players and don't get involved. My philosophy includes three things: Preparation, determination and courage, even when they're out there talking. I want to leave something for my granddaughter when I leave so that she will be able to say, 'My granddaddy worked to make San Diego a better place.'

September 10, 1971

If it takes integration to bring about quality education, then we must have integration.

April 13, 1976

Smith said that San Diego schools have made some achievements toward erasing racism and sexism … but the system still lags behind other large urban school districts.

We shouldn't have the word 'he' in our curriculum unless we really mean a he. And to look at the history books, most people still think the blue-eyed, blond-haired white man did everything for this country.

December 18, 1984

Leaders of the San Diego black community plan to demonstrate tomorrow outside the downtown federal building, against the apartheid policies of the white-dominated government of South Africa.

Apartheid is the worst form of dehumanization that exists on the planet Earth today.

July 2, 1985

Democrats seemed abuzz with anticipation last weekend when the Rev. George Walker Smith, a long-time Republican, appeared at their meeting and suggested he might become "the Jeanne Kirkpatrick of the Democratic Party." Now the minister confesses the gospel truth: *It was just a jive. I don't want a part of any party that thinks black folks have to be all in one party!*

May 8, 1986

The Catfish meetings, which are open to the public, provide members an opportunity to socialize and network – exchanging ideas and services.

We try to bring in people who can raise the level of our sensitivity and provide information that we couldn't get otherwise. We're not going to dodge any issue. We try to zero in on issues that are prevalent and far-reaching, focusing always on how it affects minorities in the community. There are very few black folk in the community who can speak out without fear of reprisal. The folk who come are here basically appreciate the fact that George Smith can say anything he wants to and not get fired. Only this church can fire me.

June 5, 1886

The Rev. George Walker Smith, a strong black voice in San Diego for 30 years, went home to Alabama and returned despondent.

I went to see my mother. She's 80 years old. Her family was once owned by a white family in South Carolina. I drove her into Montgomery from Hayneville and took her grits every morning and visited. What I saw in Montgomery makes me heartsick. I see

161

more progress for blacks there than in San Diego. A Republican mayor and George Wallace have put up a million-dollar-plus building to train unemployed blacks from four counties, and they have a 90 percent placement rate. The white folks in Montgomery are more devoted to relief of the black people than the people of San Diego.

January 31, 1987

Many black community and civic leaders could contribute to the Super Bowl effort, he said, but no attempt has been made to include them.

Why do they think only white folks in this city can accomplish anything? What efforts have been made to attract black vendors? Have there been any attempts on the part of America's Finest City to get blacks and browns and other minorities involved in the Super Bowl? No. On any Super Bowl Sunday, close to half of the players on the teams are black and they have numerous black fans. The day has passed when an event like the Super Bowl should be just a party for white folks.

Honorary doctorate, San Diego State University, 2002

Section Four
A Word in Edgewise

Chapter Thirteen
Boards & Awards

Rev. Dr. George Walker Smith has participated in the community in countless ways. Here is a partial list of his activities:

CHURCH ACTIVITIES

- Presently serving on the General Council of the Presbytery
- Elected Distinguished Alumni/ae Council of Pittsburgh Theological Seminary
- Commissioner for 3 years to the Synod of Southern California
- Association for Community Relations to the Greater Parish Ministry of San Diego (1968)
- Major Mission Committee
- Served on the Polity & Record Committee of Synod
- Served as Dean for several Junior Hi and Senior Hi Camps
- Served on the Camp & Conference Committee of the Los Angeles Presbytery
- Moderator for San Diego Presbytery

BUSINESS, CIVIC, EDUCATIONAL & PROFESSIONAL AFFILIATIONS

National:
- President, National School Boards Association, 1976
- President, Council of Great City Schools, 1972
- National Advisory Council, Educational Marketing & Research Corp
- White House Conference on Children & Youth, 1970
- Appeal Board of the National Council for Accreditation of Teacher Education
- National Advisory Commission on Juvenile Justice Y Delinquency Prevention
- White House Committee on Education & the Arts
- Board of Trustees, Pittsburgh Theological Seminary

State:
- California School Board Resolution Committee
- California School Board Association Annual State Conference Committee
- California Junior College Assoc. Committee on Student Personnel
- California Non-Partisan Voters Registration Committee
- California State Health Review & Program Council
- Ad Hoc Committee on Management of Conflict & Crime in the Schools
- California School Boards Association

Local:
- First Black to be elected to the San Diego Unified School District Board of Education, November 1963. He served four, four-year terms.
- Served as President of the Board of Education in 1966, 1970, 1977-78.
- Served as Vice-President of the Board of Education in 1965, 1969, 1976.
- Board of Trustees, San Diego, Community Colleges
- Board of Directors, Junior Achievement
- Board of Directors, Pacific Coast Bank
- Board of Directors, San Diego County Council of Boy Scouts of America
- Board of Directors, Big Brothers of San Diego, Inc
- Board of Trustees, Citizens Interracial Committee
- Advisory Board, Small Business Administration
- Capital Fund, Southeast San Diego YMCA
- Kiwanis Club of Southeast San Diego
- Black Federation of San Diego
- Smith & Associates Consultant Firm
- San Diego Urban League
- San Diego Urban Coalition
- San Diego County Citizens Scholarship Foundation
- Planetarium Authority of San Diego
- Member of San Diego Private Industry Council

- Board Member, San Diego Community College Foundation
- San Diego Crime Commission
- Planning Commission, San Diego County
- Board of Directors, San Diego County Camp Fire Girls
- Organized San Diego Chapter of O.I.C. (Opportunities Industrialization Center)
- Chairperson San Diego Area of the United Negro College Fund
- Vice President of Edmonston-Smith & Associates, a management consultant firm
- Overseers Advisory Board for the University of California at San Diego
- Board of Directors of San Diego LEAD, a leadership development program
- Member of the San Diego Black/Jewish Dialogue
- Member, Scholia Club of San Diego
- Chairman, San Diego's First Citizens Police Review Panel
- Member, Pete Wilson For Governor Committee (Local)
- Board of Directors, San Diego Innovative Preschool Project, Inc. (San Diego School of Success Preschool)
- Board of Trustees, Presbyterian Foundation
- Board of Trustees, Pittsburgh Theological Seminary
- Co-founder of Coalition for Racial Equality
- Founder and Director, Catfish Club of San Diego
- Board President, San Diego Innovative School of Success
- Organizer, Unity Day, San Diego

HONORS AND AWARDS

- San Diego's "Outstanding Young Clergyman" of the Year, 1963
- "Outstanding Young Man of America" - Junior Chamber of Comm. 1965

- "Lay Citizen Award" by Phi Delta Kappa, 1976
- Juvenile Protection Committee Award, 1965
- "Gentleman of Distinction" (Women's Guild of Temple Emanu-el)
- Brotherhood Award, National Conference of Christians & Jews, 1971
- Community & Human Relations Award, National Conference of Christians and Jews, 1972
- Headliner of the Year in Education (San Diego Press Club), 1979
- Black Achievement Award, San Diego, 1988
- YMCA Human Dignity Award (Named in honor of Dr. King) 1987
- Arco Chicano Foundation Civic Leadership Award, 1987
- Women, Incorporated Man of Achievement Award, 1987
- San Diego County Human Relations Award, 1992
- Metropolitan Fellowship Foundation Community Involvement Award, 1992
- San Diego Youth at Risk Foundation Award, 1992
- County of San Diego Sheriff Department's Appreciation Award (Named Deputy Sheriff), 1992
- CATCH Award in Appreciation for Contributions to the Residential Care Providers, 1992
- Outstanding Service/Commitment - California Youth Authority, 1993
- Sponsor/Kiwanis 6th Annual Youth Golf Tournament, 1993
- California State Senate Contributor Award to NAACP, 1993
- Special Commendation - City of San Diego for outstanding contribution for commitment to equality, 1993
- Outstanding Volunteer Service Award - Vietnam Vets, 1994
- Commitment and Dedication Award - Black Police Officers Association, 1994

- Certificate of Appreciation - San Diego Innovative Preschool of Success for vision, commitment and leadership, 1994
- SGRN Award for Community Role Model, 1994
- Commitment Award - Founder of San Diego Coalition for Equality, 1995
- Outstanding Black Educator Award - National Sorority of Phi Delta Kappa, Inc., 1995
- Tribute "A Living African American History", Palavra Tree, 1995
- Special Commendation for Community Service - City Council of San Diego, 1995
- Outstanding Community Service Award - Congressional Recognition, 1995
- Community Service Award as Founder of CATFISH Political and Social Club, 1995
- Meritorious Service Award - United Negro College Fund, 1995
- African American Leadership Award - National Panhelenic Council, 1995
- Leadership Award - Christ Church of San Diego for forty years of service to community through ministry and leadership, 1996
- Excellence In Community Service Award - American Cancer Society, 1996
- Leadership Award - San Diego Voice & Viewpoint/Gold Coast Classic, 1997
- Certificate of Appreciation - Vietnam Veterans of San Diego, 1997
- Founding Members Declaration of Honor - Sigma Pi Phi Fraternity, 1997
- IMAI Community Resource Award - KUUMBA Fest, 1997
- Certificate of Appreciation/Board Member, United Way of San Diego, 1998
- Feeling the Spirit Recognition - Museum of Photographic Arts/Chester Higgins, 1998

- Community Leader Appreciation Award - Karibu & HIV/AIDS Community, 1998
- Community Service Award/Board of Overseers/UCSD, 1999
- Youth Advocacy/Innocent Addicts Humanitarian Award
- Leadership Recognition/Named among 50 outstanding San Diegans, San Diego Magazine
- San Diego Urban League Equal Opportunity Award, 1999
- Humanitarian Award - San Diego Commandery No. 25 Knights Templar, 1999
- Community Service Appreciation Award - Rotary International, San Diego, 1999
- Boy Scouts of America Exceptional Leadership and Outstanding Service Award, 2000
- Mayoral Special Commendation for 30 years of outstanding community contributions as Leader of the Catfish Club, 2000
- Senatorial Commendation/Resolution as Leader of the Catfish Club, 2000
- Allen Temple Leadership Institute Leadership Award, Oakland, CA, 2000

Afterword

I've been privileged to work with many of San Diego's most outspoken, well-known leaders—listening and learning, while we put on paper what would inspire other San Diegans to care about our community. In my 18 years of writing about San Diego, from society galas to child abuse, never have I known a more wise and humble leader than Rev. George Walker Smith.

At first we seemed an unlikely team—how could a white woman from Los Angeles translate on paper the heart of a black man from Hayneville, Alabama? As Rev. Smith would say, God had a plan.

We have many things in common, it turns out—a seminary education, a sense of isolation from traditional institutions, a face-to-face understanding of the political process, and a love for this beautiful bayside city. The more we talked, analyzed, and swapped stories about San Diego, the more important it became to put the truth on record and let that truth seep into the hearts and minds of those who are open to dealing with it.

Rev. Smith is even more important to San Diego today than he has been as a school board president, the Catfish Club chair, or the icon of black leadership. Today his phone continues to ring, his door swings open, his counsel is sought, and his knowledge and savvy is needed more than ever to put our city on solid ground.

If we are to make the right choices in this new millennium, we need to hear his voice, absorb the mistakes of the past, admit the stupidity of racial prejudice, and break through to a new understanding of justice and equality for everyone. That's all he's really ever asked for. That's all his struggle has been about. Just equality.

During the past year, we have chuckled, been angry, and cried. Reliving pain is not an easy process. But how precious and valuable is this record of Rev. Smith's life and times for the rest of us. There will never be another like him in our midst.

Francine Phillips, 2002